TURMOIL

Robyn Williams AM, one of Australia's best-known broadcasters, has presented science programs on ABC radio and television since 1972. Early in his career he made guest appearances on *The Goodies*, *Monty Python's Flying Circus* and *Doctor Who*. The author of 16 books, he is the first journalist to be elected a fellow of the Australian Academy of Science. He was a visiting fellow at Balliol College, Oxford, and is a visiting professor at the University of New South Wales and the University of Queensland.

ROBYN WILLIAMS

TURMOIL
Letters from the brink

NEWSOUTH

A NewSouth book

Published by
NewSouth Publishing
University of New South Wales Press Ltd
University of New South Wales
Sydney NSW 2052
AUSTRALIA
newsouthpublishing.com

© Robyn Williams 2018
First published 2018

10 9 8 7 6 5 4 3 2 1

 A catalogue record for this
book is available from the
National Library of Australia

ISBN   9781742235776 (paperback)
          9781742244358 (ebook)
          9781742248806 (ePDF)

Design Josephine Pajor-Markus
Cover design Luke Causby, Blue Cork
Cover images Tom Williams and Getty Images/edge 69
Printer Griffin Press

Extract from *The Poet & The City* by W.H. Auden, first published in *The Massachusetts Review*, vol. 3, no. 3 (Spring 1962)

Contents

For Jonica.

*When I find myself in the company of scientists,
I feel like a shabby curate who has strayed by
mistake into a room full of dukes.*

— W.H. Auden

I did not expect to be here

I did not expect to be here like this. My Williams family is short-lived and I have exceeded their span by an embarrassing chunk. So here I am, in what I thought would be my twilight years, as fit and busy as ever; the brain beneath the grey thatch and the wrinkles still pretends it's 18. I'm enjoying every precious moment and look back on a life that's unfolded in a way that seems almost scripted: one golden period after another.

Until now.

Today's uncertainties were not in the script. I knew the world faced challenges, global ones, but I also knew that smart people with huge determination were ready to face them. As a society we were becoming more civilised and sensitive to others; we thought we understood the nature of his and hers, girl and boy, friend or foe, truth and lies. No more. It's a shouting match — and the good guys can't match the bullies' megaphones. Look at science. It is treated with disdain by the funders and the 'deplorables' alike. Presidents and captains of industry call climate science 'a hoax and a fraud'. Shock jocks and columnists, expert at stoking grievance, make ordinary people feel cheated. They turn decent folk into people some of us would, *yes*, be willing to deplore. Briefly.

When I was growing up they were family.

It's also hard to know when you've done well. So many friends and colleagues get fired, so many brilliant young men and women can't get jobs (unlike the way I did *in one go*, walking off the street in 1972), so many 'great leaders' become great wimps. Captains of cricket resign in tears.

And as for those political labels thrust on people as if they are a regrouping of the Bolshevik plot of a century ago, no headline or incendiary paragraph is complete without the word *left* looming like a threat to your continued wellbeing. This was one I saw, among many, in an editorial:

> … this simple undeniable truth sits at the very
> heart of the great climate change con job. Reality
> stubbornly refuses to do what the left has so
> hysterically promised and foretold it will do.

My communist father would have pissed himself with acid amusement at the genteel, mild-mannered — even earnest — souls of the scientific community being labelled as socialists, followers in the tradition of Che, Gramsci or Red Ellen. Left? Not even pink!

This is not the last act I expected, to see public discourse in this state. To see ignorance lauded and scientific research regarded as an optional 'belief'. Much worse, this is not the fate our gorgeous and largely benign civilisation deserves. The disparagement of science is an affront to the sublime beauty and complexity of the natural world that we have only recently begun to comprehend.

There is a striking disjunction in Australia. We have some tremendously talented people, young and old, keen to do good work and collaborate effectively. But we also have institutions and leadership that are, in the main, dreadful, gutless and dull. Why is this so? Should we all become New Zealanders?

The chapters that follow are reflections on this turmoil from a personal point of view. Are we facing an age of confusion and failure? A prelude to the kind of collapse that Jared Diamond writes about, but this time on a global scale? Or is this merely a short interlude, a transitory spell in the armpit of history before a new creative generation arises, no longer willing to dally with the squalor of present headlines?

These reflections focus on what may seem to be a collection of random topics: success and failure (where is the boundary between pleasure and pain?); hatred and evil (do you just give up amid the turmoil of loathing — is there a better way?); personal loss (grief can perhaps be the greatest turmoil of all); and Oxford and the Australian bush, two places I know and love and where the turmoil dissipates immediately and serenity comes quickly.

I'll admit that this is very much an attempt to convince myself that the turmoil, this age of venom and spite and ignorance, is transitory. It cannot last because it is self-destructive. People are too good. My parents were right, in their idealism at least.

In February 2017 I walked in the sunshine through the glorious campus of the University of California, Los Angeles, and watched student after student, mostly young women, walk past me with their heads down over the screens in their hands. Finally, along came one who was looking up and admiring the trees, some of which were Australian eucalypts.

'Good morning,' I said smiling, though fearing she would call the campus guards to protect her from my unwarranted intrusion. 'Why aren't you examining your phone? Why are you the only one looking at the lovely landscape?'

She smiled back, totally friendly. 'It's a beautiful morning,' she replied. 'I'm enjoying it.' I told her I'd just landed from Australia and she wished me well.

A simple encounter, but significant. A generation is beginning to look up from the tyranny of its gadgets and the confusion of its polity. Schoolkids are saying no to guns. They are turning back to books with pages. Evidence is coming in that they want to emerge to the world, if given the chance. And so, I am confident that my final personal chapter, Act Seven, is going to be OK after all. The first acts, all remarkably positive and forward looking, will not be crowned by an anomalous *crunch*.

Or am I wrong?

Turmoil and me

Few would dispute we are living through times of uncertainty and turmoil. But compared to what?

When I was born Hitler still had over a year to go. The 30th of January, my birthday, had a singular significance for Adolf because on that date in 1933 he first took ruthless charge in Germany. I was born in 1944 and World War II was in its final agonies. Although the war ended in 1945, its reverberations went on for years, even decades, in parts of the globe beyond Britain, where I lived, and in Australia. That really was turmoil.

There is something different, though, in these worrying years of 2017 and 2018 as I write. Few of us have any sense of progress, of a future direction, of how to escape what most people I talk to, especially the young, regard as a bewildering mess. Right-wing politics has managed to form some kind of strange alliance with the workers and convinced them that retail politics — the urgencies of this week's bills and upsets — is all that matters. Next year is too far off. Next decade is unimaginable. Make rage for the moment! This moment.

Turmoil. For us it seems to mean a mess without logic; without human purpose. Here come the robots. There go the jobs. And cars will drive themselves to their next appointment. Empty.

It really is tosh. But it is also, and this is the significance for me, the first time in my life that we don't have
any real sense of where we are going, and this is bad.
Turmoil today is aimless.

My own tale can be played as a series of chapters
running from an unpromising start of war, austerity
and national PTSD, to a succession of flukes: recovery,
affluence, travel, career, all accompanied by the welcome
backdrop of sex, drugs (wine) and rock 'n' roll. It looks
like a fortunate life — up till now.

*

I appeared in High Wycombe in Buckinghamshire,
where my family had evacuated to escape the London
Blitz. World War II had just over a year to go. I was
nearly evacuated in a bucket, my mother told me,
because she mistook my advent for another kind of
motion. So, the pattern was set: I'd just missed being
born in the dunny.

My life has been a beguiling succession of acts in
what can look like a drama with some lucky logic. My
parents were not married. My father Gwyn, it turns out,
had wedded someone called Elizabeth (about whom I
know nothing) in 1933, and met my mother at political
meetings. So far, so unpromising.

But then, when I was barely 15 months old, Act
One saw us escape from terrifying global conflict as the
war ended and Britain became a nation with plans to
rebuild and reform. Two years before I was born William
Beveridge produced his famous document on welfare

and the abolition of the 'giant evils' in society. Don't forget this was, incredibly, in the middle of a world war. And the Beveridge Report was taken seriously by both sides of politics. Education was transformed in schools for the lower classes (like me) by Tory minister RA Butler after *consulting the other political parties* (an Act passed when I was six months old); a national health service was conjured from the ashes of victory by the Welsh wizard Nye Bevan. Despite the political rhetoric, there seemed to be a common purpose. All this when Britain was near bankruptcy. (In 2018 Australia, despite our blatant wealth, we dare not contemplate even simple projects such as fast trains or affordable dentistry.) The rationing that had made many foods unavailable was gradually lifted and we had tangible signs of everything getting better. Stuff was in shops. We saw brightly coloured things called bananas and peaches. Austerity, on a level the present generation can only imagine, slowly faded away.

The postwar spirit lifted fast — you could feel the buzz. Even our music moved from wistful reflection to a new kind of bounce.

Act Two: 1950, we were off to Vienna. I was nearly seven. We lived in relative luxury. I learned another language and more than another culture. There were Austrians, Germans, the occupying Russians and Americans we lived with, and the countries we visited around Europe. We were so privileged. What's more I had already discovered reading. I remember at my primary school in London (or was it infants?), before Vienna, at the age of five, doing a reading test in class. Those who got the word right could go home. The first word was *piano* and I got it straightaway. Off I went. That day I discovered I could read with ease and, with the companionship of books, I could now be in a magical world forever more. Whenever I felt like it. Soon I was reading in two languages.

At the libraries in Vienna I had a random selection of books in English and German that I consumed with unswerving intensity. I have since looked up some of their titles and discovered I was reading epics such as Charles Reade's *Cloister and the Hearth* at barely eight, plenty of Maxim Gorki and Hugh Lofting and German romps such as Erich Kästner's *Emil and the Detectives* or *The Flying Classroom* in the original. Now I learn that Kästner's books had been burned by the Nazis in the 1930s.

Act Three: We returned to London. Straight to a Grammar School (thanks to RA Butler, the Tory minister, who nowadays would be taken as a Bolshevik) with old-fashioned scholarly standards and pasty 11 year olds who'd been nowhere. I was unfairly judgemental about these lads — most had barely one parent and were drastically hard up. There were two exceptions. One was David Scheuer, whose father was Czech and whose mother lived in Paris. David was, like me, bilingual. His elder brother Mike Sarne, also at the school, would go on to be a pop star and then to direct films. (His notorious version of Gore Vidal's transgender frolic *Myra Breckinridge*, starring Raquel Welch, Mae West and John Huston, is judged by some to be the worst Hollywood film in history.) David became an actor and shameless consumer of 1960s dope, dolly birds and foreign ciggies.

He would disappear to LA for mysterious frolics with the Mamas and the Papas and other sundry ravers. Grinning, he'd offer you a fag saying: 'Cancer stick?' He died of lung cancer quite young.

The other boy with some worldly poise was Michael Goldacre from Australia (Sir Henry Parkes was a relation). He was athletic, obsessed with cricket scores, came first in all subjects with no apparent effort and turned out to have a sister who looked like Brigitte Bardot. Both David and Michael became firm friends of mine and it was Michael's family who triggered my eventual escape, in 1964, to Australia.

Being in London in the years from 1955 was dull at first but there were signs of massive change. The shops were stocked once more, not lavishly, with exotic produce. Immigrants from India and the West Indies brought strange fruit such as avocados and spices that most of us had not seen before. Cars looked somehow brighter and sleeker, not so boxy and rough. Our clothes became less lumpy and endlessly repaired as new fabrics appeared to make us look fresh and ready. Then: Elvis. And Bill Haley. And their British imitators Tommy Steele and Guy Mitchell. The late 1950s ended with glorious uproar.

Then it was the 1960s and The Beatles and a sweep of exuberance and creativity took hold that came with a new optimism, a conviction that almost anything was possible. And it was.

Act Four: Oz! An odd time, you would guess, to up sticks and travel, alone, age 20, to distant Australia. But I was escaping deep poverty. My family, what was left of it, had no income. I had hitchhiked around Europe every year with friends David Scheuer and Michael Goldacre, sleeping on beaches or in vineyards. We spoke French and German and knew how to negotiate foreign parts and be 'on the road'. Jack Kerouac had shown us the romance of travel without a dollar and we imagined ourselves to be the European equivalent: troubadours on Route Nationale Sept, the highway leading to the south of France — basically schoolkids on a cheap vacation in search of sex, but in our imaginations we were on an adventure, pursuing exotic delights. Eating little but grapes and cheese for days on end in no way blunted our spirits.

So, the next big challenge was to do the same globally. My mates all promised to come with me to Australia, but one by one dipped out. Leaving me alone with a ten-pound ticket — the special fare available to intending migrants — on the *Castel Felice* sailing from Southampton in 1964. Despite my ticket, I planned to stay in Australia for just two years, saving lots of that fortune you could earn working on the Snowy Scheme, then hitchhiking from Sydney to London. When the ship docked at Pyrmont in Sydney I had two problems. The first was that my documents insisted I was female (the Welsh spelling of Robyn did it) and second, I had nowhere to live and no job.

The man from the migrant assistance outfit (called Big Brother — seriously!) solved the first problem by taking out a biro and crossing out Miss on my documents and remaking me male by writing Mr. (Were today's gender uncertainties so simply solved!) He next dealt with the second difficulty by announcing I was to live in 'Mosman' off Military Road and go to work at the Repatriation Department. I had visions of a distant barracks off a troop route somewhere in the distant bush and was astounded to find myself at the harbour end of Raglan Street in Sydney's poshest suburb blessed with the best views on Earth. And the job was not some horrid exercise in transnational deportation but a clerical task, calculating pensions for old soldiers. What's more, the Repatriation office in the Grace building (now a swank hotel) turned out to be three minutes from the Royal George pub, favourite of the Push. It was the 1960s drinking HQ for bohemian icons such as Germaine Greer, Richard Neville, PP McGuinness, Robert Hughes and many more. My luck was holding.

*

I was able to scoot off to Oz in 1964 because I was free. My father had died in 1962. My mother was housebound and broken.

Gwyn Williams seems now like a stern ghost from an old film made in Wales. He was born barely in the twentieth century, in 1905, and I last saw him alive 55 years ago. I've tried to find people who knew him but most of those have gone too. There are few traces left.

What I know is this: he was handsome, clever, athletic, sang in Welsh, was a coal-miner from age 14, became a mining engineer at 17, a trade union leader and a spy (amateur in the extreme) in the 1950s. He had a formidably strong personality that used to scare me shitless. I was secretly glad to hear he'd died at only 57. Isn't that shameful? But I was *free*. In one bound.

I now remember some good things about him. I loved lying in bed on weekend mornings with my parents (I must have been five or six) as he sang songs in his confident tenor voice. I was reminded of this when, in 2016 in Swansea, I visited the house where Dylan Thomas was born. I recorded my tour with Steve, who'd restored the small home on the steep hill, for ABC Radio. Our conversation lasted over an hour and for me was almost like an exuberant trance as memories came back. The lovely Welsh accents and lilting phrases; Steve put an ancient LP onto a record player with a real horn, like in the movies, and over the scratches and crackles came a song my father used to sing, 'Sosban Fach', about a little saucepan, and though I hadn't heard it for over half a century, I *began to sing along with it*. Something was embedded. Those songs, that Welsh language. The program, ostensibly an 'archaeology of Dylan Thomas' for *The Science Show*, was heard by some who know me as my 'goodbye' program. But it wasn't a farewell, more a celebration of memories of youth.

Gwyn was also an idealist and a communist. He had taken on a few of the favourite phrases from the Stalinist claptrap of his age, but he didn't take them seriously. Even amid the turmoil of his adult life — the Depression, World War II and the Cold War — he still believed in some sort of Promised Land. It was only towards the end, ruined by the tiny conspiracies of the tinier circle of comrades, an irrelevant rump left behind as the world changed, that he faltered; his once strong body wrecked by miner's diseases, his spirit gave up. I am now 17 years older than my old man was when he died. Strange feeling.

As a spy his career was brief and, apparently, ineffectual. I'd love to see his files from MI5. I gather there were three of them, mainly because the spooks kept getting his name wrong. There was one for George Williams, one for Gwyn and one for Gwynfor. In September 2017, I happened to meet a young student in Sussex who was investigating a history of one of my father's unions, that of the scientists, and I was told that there is much material about him at Warwick University. I can't see myself trekking there to investigate. What could I find? Acres of old print about quixotic plans and tedious meetings. In Vienna, Gwyn was assigned to something called the WFTU (World Federation of Trade Unions) housed in an old palace in the centre. I thought and knew little about it until a couple of years ago when I read Le Carré's book *Absolute Friends* and there were the familiar initials WFTU, likened by Le Carré to a communist front organisation. As I remember it, it had all the airs and graces of a mini United Nations. Plenty of pricey drinks under the huge chandeliers.

My mother, Ray (Rachel) Davies, was a complete contrast to Gwyn. So much so that I can't imagine how they coexisted intimately for so long without murdering each other, let alone conceiving and raising three children.

She too was athletic, more a bundle of muscle in her younger days: trim and strong, with an Eastern European face and black hair in rising waves from a widow's peak as they liked to perm it in those 1940s and 1950s styles. She too was mysterious in her family provenance.

My late brother Shwn tried to research it when he lay dying in his hospital bed, a laptop on the crumpled sheets. The records from Lvov in Poland, he found, were all gone. The 'Davies' family that eventuated in the East End of London in the 1920s (?) had a variety of surnames and I lost track of Ray's brothers who bore them. She seemed uninterested in her family and its heritage beyond the lives of her own children and our exploits until her health collapsed.

Ray was a natural linguist and lateral thinker. Her brain could jump and make humorous connections that would often leave listeners mystified. I find I have similar foibles, a brain like an electric grasshopper, and there are only a few familiars who are able to deconstruct my jokes or references to exasperated bystanders, offering them links I've assumed are obvious. I, and Ray, perfected the allusion from nowhere. (These days Jonica has assumed the burden of being my interpreter.)

When I told my mother I was off to Australia in 1964 she was saddened but couldn't stop me. She was agoraphobic and housebound. Her cosmopolitan zest and love of the Continent were quashed forever. Like Gwyn, she had been marooned in the twilight zone. I was to carry the torch on her behalf, she told me. The promise of untold wealth to be earned in the Snowy placated her somewhat.

*

Act Five: The ten-quid trip to Oz, as I indicated, was a con. I had no intention of staying. It was a way to get to the other side of the planet, then hitchhike the Big One, back home after the required two years' stay, accomplishing a venture that would become commonplace in the 1960s and 1970s as many a hairy youth ventured to India and beyond in search of enlightenment. I duly set out from North Sydney station in August 1966 aiming to reach Piccadilly in mid-December. This was achieved on the dot (18 December!) and I arrived with an Australian wife called Pamela. We had heard the new Beatles LP *Revolver* in a record shop in Kuala Lumpur and hit London just a couple of months before the explosive release of *Sgt. Pepper's* and all that came with it.

I enrolled in a Bachelor of Science degree at the University of London. My university years were coupled with television appearances from 1966 to 1971 thanks to Pamela, who was working as a casting director for ATV and Lew Grade and the BBC. (Her first series was *The Prisoner* starring Patrick McGoohan.) She helped me get a couple of agents who would provide a variety of gigs from costume dramas and cop shows to *Monty Python*, *The Goodies*, and four months as a stand-in for Tom Jones. Life consisted of sitting in the audience seats in big TV studios trying to write essays on xylem and phloem transport in ancient plants or the classification of bony fish and suddenly being required to take Tom's script as he went off to make-up (or something in the caravan with one of the dancers!) and rehearse the sketch for his variety show with Peter Sellers, or Cher, or Terry-Thomas, and then back I went to botany or dogfish parts.

I had five years of that kind of utterly contrasting life: one day with the *Monty Python* team on location, the next sitting in a monumentally tedious lecture on the evolution of ferns.

It seemed random, basic biology plus 1960s showbiz, but it was a perfect preparation for science broadcasting. That started, for me, in early 1972, in time for the closing of the Apollo era. On what was supposed to be a brief trip back to Sydney, I walked off the street into the ABC just as the last two sets of men prepared to go to the moon. Pamela had wanted to see her family again and we were intending to stay for 12 months. ABC Science had a fluke vacancy and I was there to do the slog work as a gopher to help those on air present the live broadcasts from the moon for Apollo 16 in April and the final adventure, Apollo 17, in December. One day in April I was jolted from sending messages into the studio with bits of research for the on-air people to talk about whenever the astronauts took a break. The founder of ABC Science, Peter Pockley, was hosting the broadcast and had been on air for hours, probably since before dawn. Then, during a news break, he simply left the 'live' studio, told me which switches to press and said: 'Take over.' I had two minutes' notice and survived. I can't remember what I said — something prosaic, no doubt — but I was now a broadcaster. How did all that happen?

Act Six: The ABC kept me on and another Act unfolded. I did the lot: radio, TV, print, the first phone-ins on ABC Radio. We were even allowed to venture on to commercial networks. (Or were we? I don't recall asking permission.) It was a magnificent training.

Science was in its second postwar phase, following Kennedy and the space race, an era when Australian research was taking off and the revolutions of genomes and genetic engineering and the human history of this southern land and much more were reaching new levels of discovery and meaning.

It seemed all set. A smooth growth to greater riches and insights and, who knows, peace on Earth. After Woodstock came the Age of Aquarius and Alternative Australia in places such as Nimbin in northern New South Wales and pleasant pastures near Perth and so on. Once you removed the flake and the hash you found a generation with a genuine concern about building a better future. This was not much reflected in orthodox politics, and Barry Jones, soon to be a minister for science in the Hawke government, was moved to call his book on what was possible *Sleepers, Wake!*, after William Blake's entreaty for everyone to open their eyes to a fresh reality.

And, yes, science and technology everywhere did flourish and achievements were spectacular. But the link to social goals has never been set clearly and confidently in the public mind, let alone mainstream politics. Science meant funding and funding means taxes. Taxes are *bad*. So it went on for decades as our leaders gloried in the successes but ducked when they needed to pay for them — even though they paid for themselves. And now we have a standoff. Turmoil.

But in the midst of public turmoil, my personal Act Seven included unexpected joy. My marriage to Pamela had run its course; the kids were grown up and she had met a terrific guy, a conductor called Christopher Bowen. I had been abroad a lot with a couple of fellowships at Oxford and reporting assignments. That's when Jonica appeared — another fluke in this apparently charmed life.

Joy

The call came 24 years ago from a producer with the ABC morning show in Melbourne. He said I should call Dr Jonica Newby: she did bits on video and TV about animals and she was smart, talented and — all chaps say this — gorgeous. So I did. Call her.

I have always looked for members of the public who may be able to do something I can broadcast. We are the Australian *Broadcasting* Corporation after all, the public broadcaster. The simplest way for folk to join in, even now, is to write a script. You don't need gear for that, no microphones or cameras; just words. Good words.

Jonica, when I eventually met her (she was 28), obviously had good words. It came from a lifelong habit of reading books. Like me, she spends two to three hours every day reading. This gives her a clarity of expression and a command of material that translates to print, radio, TV or any other of your online thingummies proliferating everywhere. The fundamental requirement for journalism is language. The rest follows.

Jonica began with a few vignettes about dogs and cats. Each offering improved on the one before. We discussed bigger matters, beyond furry pets, and I found she had ideas about why we are so close to other creatures, how we evolved together and whether they helped domesticate us, as well as the other way around.

This led to a series of *Science Show*s on the nature of animal attraction. It showed how, as humans, we may have been able to depend on dogs to hunt with us, and how some scientists speculated that our very form may have developed in a more gracile way, with a less robust skull structure, more mobile mouths and finer limbs, because we could delegate the hard stuff to our new mates. Our companion hunters, dogs, also had fabulous alarm systems with more powerful eyes and noses to alert the camp. So, we evolved, the theory went, like puppies, to mature earlier and so retain youthful characteristics. We did not need such big jaws and heavy limbs. This is called neoteny. At this time, in the early 1990s, Bob Wayne, professor of genetics at UCLA, was also putting dog history way back at 100 000 years (as I have written elsewhere, this figure has now been reduced to 40 000 years). This seemed to suggest we had been together, dog and human, nearly forever. All good stuff for conjecture — and the series gave for and against, as you would expect when any such provocative material surfaced.

Jonica relished the challenge, did interviews, wrote scripts as if she'd done it all her life, and met deadlines like a pro.

I have often used short talks as the basis for expansion for writers to do series: from Derek Denton to Peter Mason (famously), Jane Goodall (University of Western Sydney), Mark Dodgson, Anne Deveson, Tony Barnett and many more, to grow into major broadcasters. They are often taken up by other networks. Jonica's series of

*Science Show*s was *The Pact for Survival*, broadcast in 1997.

Jonica was soon invited by the then executive producer of ABC TV Science, Jeune Pritchard, to do a series matching our radio one. By this stage Jonica had moved into my house in Balmain, Termite Towers. I had never imagined we could possibly become an item. She was, and still is, 23 years younger than I am. I was established with a grown-up family; my wife Pamela and I had been together for 32 years but, as the cliché goes, had developed somewhat separate lives. I tend not to be pushy when it comes to my relationships with women (sometimes exasperating them) and, after a year of knowing Jonica, and having had innumerable dinners together discussing ethology and ABC politics, one night I dared to ask whether she really had to go home. She didn't.

We have been together ever since. Happily.

Since Jonica and her *Catalyst* colleagues were fired from the ABC without ceremony in 2016, a cull that continues pitilessly all over the organisation to this day, she has used her own savings to try to make a film about climate and the 'end of winter'. This has taken her to California and Colorado, carrying her own camera. Real TV broadcasters these days (there are some, just) can direct, produce and, like Jonica, shoot their own sequences while reporting. It matches the new austerity experienced everywhere as social technologies compete with traditional forms. Do those executives who've never made a program realise that people like Jonica reduce their costs spectacularly? Apparently not. Now is the time, surely, for all-rounders. If you can handle nearly all media, you can think creatively. You can combine vision with music, storytelling with ideas and know when to take some of it to go on the net or YouTube. Remember that three-minute extract from the piece on *Catalyst* on cancer and exercise? Since released on Facebook it has scored 31 million views.

That's why a well-run ABC is so important for nurturing rare talent. It has been my delight to see younger program-makers, most of them women, bounce off each other with enthusiasm, daring and a willingness to share their ideas. In the commercial world, the name of the game is the *pitch*. You bid, you sell, you try to impress the market, usually in the form of a louche guy with an attention deficit. The result is invariable disappointment and conventional shows. Many parts of the ABC are being moved in this top-down direction.

So now we are in unfamiliar territory. Professionally, that is. I have no idea where Jonica's next job will come from. I do remember when, 20 years ago, she was offered an executive role overseas running a firm's interests in South-East Asia for a starting salary of $400 000 plus perks. She turned it down to do her *Science Show* series instead. With a relaxed shrug.

I can't think of many I've known in this complicated world who would give mammon the flick with such exquisite assurance.

In many ways Jonica represents the woman of the twenty-first century: hugely intelligent, qualified in so many ways, kind and thoughtful, with enormous potential, yet ignored and treated with contempt by those galloping mediocrities now so widely In Charge.

How can a major nation hope to reach new heights of excellence when it treats people so poorly?

On a personal level I am eternally pleased I answered that call from Melbourne. What if I hadn't? A case of *Sliding Doors*? For someone almost allergic to picking up a ringing phone I must have been in a particularly serene mood that day. Thank the stars!

Shit

Of all the cancers I could pick, I knew I'd end up with bowel cancer. Call it colon, if you like, bowdlerise it, make it appear more seemly, more Paddington Bear, more … *nice*. But bowels mean shit and shit means stinky and poo. How could you try to be romantic carrying a colostomy bag? One that burst last week? In the office!

I had been passing blood. Most of us men ignore such things. Make up some excuse such as a bleeding haemorrhoid, though we know full well there are no piles up there, bleeding or otherwise.

Time passed. I promise I will have a week of doctors later in the year: teeth, piles, asthma, throat. Teeth are fixed, expensively. Asthma goes away. Throat turns out to be acid reflux, like my dad's, probably from a hiatus hernia, and its consequences gave my brother oesophageal cancer and he died of it, uncomplaining for once to the very end. Having seen an ENT specialist I'm told I must give up wine, take pills every day, use an extra pillow. I eschew the first two and settle for the last.

Piles turn out to be Not Piles. As the doctor sends me off for a colonoscopy I think of the French word for batteries and laugh. The test involves drinking enormous glugs of foul liquid tasting like gorilla fart. Then I have botty-cam, just like the willy-cam they gave me in 1991 when I had bladder cancer. I quite like that: the anaesthetic and delicious sense of dropping off as you go to the Land of Nod. But the camera up the freckle is easier and the unconsciousness somehow swifter.

And then I'm told, barely awake again, that I have two tumours, a 5 millimetre and 3 millimetre, and it's they who've been bleeding. Copiously. And must come out. With lots of gut. I am lobbed to a surgeon. He is young and Asian–Australian and efficient. He tells me the chop must be next week (*But I've got appointments!* I yell) and that thereafter I shall no longer be able to shit like a young fellow: he says I'll no longer be able to do one big 'dump' every day in the morning like most chaps do, but lots of little craps instead. He doesn't tell me that some of them will give about two seconds notice and sometimes give the alarm nine times a night.

I went for the chop a few days later. Jonica came with me and explained to the surgeon both my habit of making jokes, even minutes before theatre and, as she's known me for 20 years, what those jokes meant. I can be slightly cryptic with newcomers. She translated.

The surgeon got his own back after the op. 'Do I still have a rectum?' I asked.

'No,' he replied, deadpan. 'It's in my bucket under the sink.' He meant every word.

I had been making, as usual, arrangements for work and play to resume within days of my colectomy. The surgeon gave wise advice: 'It's like being hit by a truck. You'll need lots of rest to recover.' I took seven days.

The ABC, as usual, played sympathetic but I was suspicious that their solicitude, at least in management, was more concerned with avoiding legal liabilities if I fell over, rather than warm concerns about my wellbeing. This was confirmed when, two months after the op, I had my trip to the USA cancelled, something I'd been working on for months. It included a visit to the University of British Columbia in Vancouver, the campus where I'd started *The Science Show* 40 years before. With three days to go the ABC cancelled my permission, saying they could not get me insured even though I had two letters from doctors saying I was fit to work.

I told the ABC I'd go anyway, taking leave and paying for myself. This I did. When I returned, carrying more interviews than ever before, I was given some of my money back. I wrote something astringent to the HR person who had pulled the plug, someone I'd never met. As a result I was required to give her a personal apology for doubting her goodwill. I have since been amused to note that no one from what is now chummily called ABC People has since asked, even casually, how I may be faring. It is easy to infer that our personnel outfit, like those in many modern corporations, is there primarily to watch for the interests of the firm, not its employees. Watch out for the legalities. Odd that, in 47 years and after three fatal diseases (bladder cancer in 1991 and cardiac arrests in 1988) no 'personnel' officer has come downstairs to ask 'How are you?' just out of curiosity. The evidence is compelling.

One mishap occurred on the Sydney to Los Angeles leg of my journey to Vancouver. I'd upgraded myself with points and was lying asleep on my flat bed when a steward shook me awake. 'Body fluids,' he whispered, confusingly. Was I leaking? How could they tell? I was raised and asked to move across the aisle. I explained I had a bag and it was under control but could leak sometimes from the effects of chemo. A stewardess arrived. She was a nurse and tremendously reassuring. She stripped me down to my knickers and set about repairing the bag's attachment to my right-hand side, just to the east of my belly button. She used up half a roll of tape and quickly pronounced me fit for duty. Her performance was so cheery and medically professional that I later wrote to Alan Joyce, CEO of Qantas, praising her brilliance. No passenger was disturbed.

That should have been the end of the episode — but not quite. As we approached the coast of the USA we were told by the captain that fog had closed LA and we were heading to Ontario. *Canada?* I thought — but no, this was a town in California. We landed to wait for the all-clear. My plans to run to the first-class lounge as we changed planes to go to Vancouver fell apart. There would be no chance to clean up. I found a new plane ticket waiting and continued the trek rather soiled. The man sitting next to me seemed not to notice.

The point about this malady is that it takes so much effort. Like babies, there is no down time. And there's shit everywhere. You clean up and wipe incessantly. And hide all signs of it from view.

A few months later we stopped the chemo. It was making me lose weight on a troubling scale, and colleagues were getting spooked by a bent cadaver, me, working away in their midst and firmly denying being unwell. Finally Jonica frogmarched me back to hospital. My weight had descended below hers, and she's a sylph, so it was time to be reconnected to my lower intestine — time to try shitting again.

The month in hospital was trying. I was told to 'think of myself and recovery, not work', but I needed at least two hours of reading or other intellectual engagement every day to avoid feeling like an exhausted overcooked Brussels sprout. Once I even did an interview while in the ward, with the editor-in-chief of *Nature*, no less, Sir Philip Campbell. Without fuss, he came into the hospital instead of the ABC studios (small diversion) and talked about *Nature* journals in Australia. Two visitors arrived in the middle of this and I barked hoarsely 'Not yet!' and they ducked out. When back at the ABC I revoiced the questions to make up for my thin tones and Sir Philip went to air.

Nowadays I have put on the missing kilos and look normal. The cancer seems to have gone away, but you never know. The real miracle, apart from the marvellous support from Jonica and ex-wife Pamela and other friends, has been *exercise*.

*

Have you seen Edith Cowan recently? She's on the $50 note and resplendent there with parted grey hair and a wistful look. She was the first woman to be elected to an Australian parliament. A university is named after her, the only one in the country named after a female achiever, and despite its youth (barely 36 years) it is already making a significant mark.

Professor Rob Newton runs an exercise gym there, right next to the chemo ward. Patients get their drugs and fierce workouts *at the same time*. Well, quickly one after the other.

I did an interview with patients and staff and was deeply impressed by the evidence. Research from there and in Europe was showing that vigorous training speeds recovery and makes treatment more effective. We already knew that exercise improves the workings of most organs of the body. Why? Because it mobilises macrophages, the cleaning cells that mop up waste, clearing brains, kidneys, livers and much else to get on with life. Imagine any machine crammed with crud and you'll realise pretty quickly it won't perform efficiently. Same with the body. It is built for action.

Jonica followed up my brief radio effort with a major half-hour investigation for *Catalyst* on ABC TV. It is still there for you to see, if you can put up with my thin visage and blotchy torso. (That's *before recovery!*) She marshalled the evidence from Danish labs and the Karolinska Institute in Stockholm and from Edith Cowan and found a compelling story. It was reinforced by the bewildering neglect: hardly anywhere had cancer treatment been examined in tandem with exercise, and what is even more perplexing, cancer itself is hardly taught at all as part of the basic medical degree in Australia. Ben Bravery in Melbourne, himself a sufferer from bowel cancer at the age of 28, appeared on Radio National's *Ockham's Razor* in March 2017 saying he's now three years into a medical course and cancer hardly has a mention. I ran this (being somewhat incredulous myself) past Dr Norman Swan before broadcast, and he nodded agreement.

Cancer with exercise, the teaching about both in medical courses, both missing.

After I finished my own treatment and shed nearly all drugs (I was being made to swallow 55 tablets a day in hospital), Jonica found me a delightful trainer in Balmain, where we live. Jacquie is qualified scientifically, in pathology, and knows what resistance training you need to mobilise the adrenaline which turns out to be the stimulant for bodily juices that zap potential tumours. Once a week I do exercises I don't normally fancy — we all settle for comfortable runs and sit-ups rather than those irksome routines that really make a difference. When I left hospital I felt thin, flat and old; Jonica promised me that, after constant workouts I'd be better than before the operations. She's right. Once a year I run the length of Seven Mile Beach. I feel slightly weary during the last quarter mile.

Others I know have been to see Jacquie to try the Edith Cowan regime. One is a former vice-chancellor and she is thrilled by the results. So are others I've sent.

But I still get caught short. That abbreviated gut and absence of a rectum! Once I was at a university in London doing an interview with a famous professor. He was beginning to wind up when I felt a belly alert. Was it wind? Or the real thing? I let him finish — but then he had another thought. He continued at length

with caveats and illustrations and then an addendum.
Which was when I found out it was not wind.

Repairs in the loo below took 20 minutes. This happens once a month. Beware late dinners and farty food. But most good fibrous food causes wind — such as my favourite, Brussels sprouts. Another bind is loss of sleep, especially when the ABC is in dire straits, which is all the time. You wake at 2 a.m. for a pit stop and promise not to think about the latest managerial affront, and fail: frenzied thoughts last until dawn.

But it is good not to be dead, despite the shits. They get under control gradually and steadily. You pass through the nappy stage in four to five months, then ease into something resembling normal life. And romance continues. Even the squeamish eventually manage with grace. And the science continues, thrillingly. Not just exercise and microbiomes, but the IQ in your belly: the guts have as many nerves as the brain and they are there to do a job. People survive well and can control their destiny ... up to a point.

I am reminded of the advice an outrageous older woman used to give to her male friends when they passed seventy years of age:

Never waste an erection.

Never trust a fart.

Never pass a public toilet in the hope that you'll get away with it.

Politics and the media

As we flounder in this barren political landscape, our media do all they can to foment fear and loathing. I self-flagellate every day by reading all the shouty newspapers and listening to most radio. There are the headlines constantly smearing left-wing conspiracies and green outrages. The shock-jock style of Rush Limbaugh has become commonplace; a river of hate and disparagement runs from Fox News to the Murdoch press and much more, all day every day. I remember when the new Chief Scientist, Dr Alan Finkel, was appointed in early 2016, the Sydney *Daily Telegraph* waited just two days before plastering his photoshopped picture on the front page, depicting him as a clowning hippie with headband and beads — all to ridicule his comments on the possibilities of green energy. The newspapers are little more than propaganda sheets and words like 'left wing', 'tax-payer funded', 'elites' and 'expert' are constant insults. Even now 'inner-city type' as disparagement reminds me very much of the way 'international type' was once used as code for 'dirty Semite' in *Der Stürmer*.

When a petition was made public protesting against the New South Wales State Government's proposal to hoist the Powerhouse Museum on trucks and transport it to Parramatta at a cost of over $1 billion, the *Daily Telegraph* put one of the signatories, Cate Blanchett, on its cover with accompanying invective. Inside the paper was a large map of the city with other signatories' faces placed over their privileged suburbs — the 'inner-city types' were conspiring once more to disadvantage ordinary citizens in the outer suburbs and the bush.

A constant bombardment like this has its effect. Especially in a world suffused with uncertainty. Yellow journalism has been around for generations. Some media moguls even boasted about being able to start wars to back up the propaganda in their papers that masquerades as proper copy. Now it is both more shrill and reinforced by social media material shown to be manipulated on a huge scale. Cambridge Analytica has even boasted of its role in having Trump elected. Is it surprising that voters have served up slop instead of potentially strong and effective governments?

And the ABC? Well, it has descended into self-conscious self-protection, not so much in its programs (the comedies such as *Last Leg* and *Mad as Hell* are especially forthright) but in its management. As usual this is a haphazard affair with some departments as brave and professional as ever, while others can be abject in their attempts to downplay comments about climate or to risk offending financial interests. This situation is worse in 2018 because the ABC is top down in a way I find greater than ever before. They also manage by email — so you may never meet the instructor from above, only the faux-cheery order. One has images of agitated suits, most of them innocent of any real creative experience as writers or producers, sent into spasms like dancing brolgas as the latest ABC bashing erupts, furiously crafting the standby message for the troops below. All in the cause of self-protection as the outside world continues to attack this 'tax-payer funded enclave' in its 'inner-city compound' drinking lattes at the expense of Struggle Street.

Which is pointless, of course. The more the enforcement grows, the more inefficient and army-like the ABC becomes. One enlightened senior executive, now departed, told me that if he had been selected as the new director of ABC TV his first action would have been to gather the staff together, pile up 80 per cent of the combined paperwork on rules and regulations and set it on fire. To the applause, no doubt, of all present.

*

Australia was once known to the bewildered Europeans as the Topsy-Turvy Land, where the world was upside down, the 'deer' hopped and birds hung sideways from branches screeching blue murder. Now we have the same with politics. Even in America. Factory workers without jobs vote for flagrant billionaires; Mr and Mrs Ordinary, whose middle-of-the-road political choices were as predictable as rain in Melbourne, now choose the candidates who want to invade North Korea ... or anywhere; and everybody screeches blue murder. And achieves very little.

Politics is a noisy sport with winners and losers. Right now it has nothing to do with governing. (It *does* in most of Europe, New Zealand and Canada, countries with different traditions.)

So what about left versus right? Is it really so old-fashioned? Do you know the class sketch from the David Frost TV show 50 years ago? It caricatured the three classic British classes: tall John Cleese, wearing a bowler hat, was the toff; Ronnie Barker was in the middle in his bourgeois homburg, looking up to Cleese; and tiny Ronnie Corbett in his proletarian cloth cap was dwarfed by both. Cleese was, of course, 'upper class', Barker 'middle class' and Corbett 'knew his place'.

By implication the toff voted Tory, for Maggie or Menzies; in the centre Ronnie Barker was a middle-brow, middle-of-the-road swinging voter: Lib-Dem or even Green, occasionally Conservative (why not?), Liberal in Oz. Traditional Tory was noblesse-oblige and rather comfy — or so it seemed back then. But there was no doubt about the fellow who 'knew his place': Labour. Always. In the USA, Democrat. In Australia, Labor. Rusted on, as they used to say.

Could they have swapped hats 50 years ago, jumped their respective class and party allegiances? Well, yes, up to a point, Lord Copper. Even then the middle man in the sketch, Barker, confessed he was richer than the toff. They could have exchanged hats and Barker would have looked fine in Cleese's bowler. But the horny-handed son of toil? Conservative? Not likely. And in a bowler he'd have looked like a bollard — not even manly outside his place in the line-up. Worker meant left wing.

Go to YouTube and watch the sketch. It is still telling. But now in 2018 the two Ronnies are dead and voting patterns are berserk.

What makes a class, if such still exists in America

or Australia, vote against its own clear interests? One answer has been emotion: in your rage against neglect you don't perceive a real choice, a sensible selection, and, instead, you go in for revenge. The split-second buzz of loathing as you say bollocks to the establishment. The elite. There is also the upheaval in manufacturing jobs: the car industry, mining (my father's trade). But there are other explanations.

One is the leap of history.

In Australia I am convinced we skipped a generation by mistake. When Kevin Rudd became leader of the Labor Party he replaced a man who had vast experience in government and deep expertise in at least two aspects of it, defence and foreign affairs: Kim Beazley. Kim also knew plenty about education policy and finance. He was a rounded politician, erudite and calm. Perhaps too much calm, which some took as indolence. What's more he was a Balliol graduate. Rudd, on the other hand, was too raw, too untested, managerially febrile. Meanwhile, on the Tory (Liberal) side, the man who should have led the party after so many years in the shadow of John Howard, the toreador meant to be ready to mount the leader's stallion, was Peter Costello. But Costello said no.

He did not fancy running about in a smaller ring in Opposition away from the crowds, having strutted so well in the Big One, albeit during easier times when the money rolled into the exchequer without pause and Australia had it easy. So he fled to Collins Street.

Our two main parties had skipped a generation, lost the leaders with deep experience and, politically, we have been out of sync ever since. Government, such as it is, has been a continuing embarrassment, improvising, reacting, offering zingers and slogans instead of thought and action. No wonder one's vote seems something to squander. What's the point? Nothing seems to be achievable in a turbulent world where everything needs to be done urgently to plan for a secure future.

And in America: the same tale with different origins. I don't wish to expose any left-wing biases but … just look at the line-up of Republican presidents following that real statesman, Dwight Eisenhower. You have Nixon, Reagan, Bush and Bush and now the Donald. A crook followed by a buffoon, then a grey bush and a thick bush. And now a freak. By the way, don't tell me Ronnie Reagan was a success, go back and look at the overspending, the number of his team who ended up in jail and the fiasco of Star Wars. Ronnie 'retired to the White House'. All of them, all those dodgy men, could fit into the White House perfectly well *because they didn't have to do anything*. To quote Ronnie: '… government is not the solution to the problem; government is the problem.' That's why Donald is fine. Like Peter Sellers in the film *Being There*, he can simply sleepwalk through the presidential routine while making rude noises. Modern conservatism is a snack: secure the borders, cut the taxes, elevate the family (while playing up when you think no one is looking) and the rest just happens. If things get tricky just bomb somebody.

One of the reasons I am not left wing is that I have so many hard-right mates. Some are in the family. When I ask them about the shambles of American politics they say two things. First, the Constitution is set up so that the president can hardly do anything beyond go to war. Fears of another Oliver Cromwell or even a Mad King George made the Founding Fathers ensure that the constraints on the man in the White House are so severe he is lucky to be able to say God Bless America let alone save health care. And what about the blatant gerrymander of the states, favouring Republicans in a way that makes the rotten boroughs of nineteenth-century England look quaint?

So, it's all really fine, say my right-wing interlocutors because, secondly, the useful activity takes place all over, outside Washington DC and the constraints of government, local or national, as clever chaps in smoke-filled rooms and golf courses get things done anyway, out of sight. That's why government must be small, yet retain the public ritual of speechifying and Senate inquiries to make it look like democracy is taking place. But the real powers are invisible in America. Unless you know.

I have long wondered about the paradoxes of both modern conservatism and modern terrorism because both seem so nihilistic. The Republicans refused to cooperate with charming, naive Obama from Day One, on anything, even at the risk of destroying government itself, because it didn't matter to them if that happened: if small government is good, no government (beyond the folderol) is best. As for terrorists, they couldn't care less about the mayhem and misery they create in the world because this life is pointless; only the next life matters.

Both bomb throwers and hardliners have an easy policy: destruction. They are nihilists. And so we encounter once more the twenty-first-century voter, without a choice that makes any sense, so you just write bollocks on your form. Brexit bollocks, Donald bollocks or Hanson bollocks. What's the difference?

*

The blight that unites both left and right in 2018 is an absence of any sense of the future. They have been told that retail politics is what counts — the prices in the shops and on your bills, hospital and GP visits, transport, what happens next Tuesday, not next decade. Tony Abbott exclaimed in late 2016 that his successor's pronouncements on 'agility and innovation' meant little to the electorate.

Is this because a vision of a better society is lacking or because modern Australians and others reject foresight? I suspect it is because politicians are offering slogans about the future (and everything else), not firm projections based on authoritative advice. Compare the attitude of Paul Keating when he was prime minister. I had dinner with him soon after he took office. He was keen to talk about how we science journalists were trying to 'educate' Australians in our daunting field of expertise. He said his own task was to do the same with economics. He knew it would take a long time and he persevered, eventually winning the respect of the nation, both left and right. We knew it was important, we knew that the ham-fisted approach of yesteryear had to change and that reform was essential, in everybody's interest. It was courageous and it was real leadership.

Australians right now have no sense of where they are heading. The utopian dreams of the old socialists and the hippie sixties crowd have faded; there will be no communes or workers' paradises spreading across the wide brown land. No singing of 'Kumbaya' or red flags. What then?

Plenty. It is perfectly possible to marshal all the opportunities of new cities: clean transport, no waste, brilliant schools, superbly green cheap housing and rewarding twenty-first-century jobs. We report on these ingredients all the time. There are masses of bright ideas. Just put them together in a coherent strategy and then show how you can get there. This can be done by a combination of idealism (call it 'left' if you really want to) and hard-headed free-enterprise realism.

It is not happening because the real left has lost its nerve and now resorts to spoiling politics and the real right never had much nerve and insists on seeing foresight as a mixture of Soviet-style Five Year Plans and nanny-state meddling. This leaves the citizens of Australia, the UK and the USA floundering, with nowhere to go but the cash register. It's not surprising that they have become cynical in the face of tribal politics where winning is all that counts.

*

Which brings me to three quotations in closing. The first is from Charles Darwin, who said: 'Ignorance more frequently begets confidence than does knowledge.' This explains not only the confidence with which many of we public broadcasters are trashed by those who don't listen to our programs, but also the relative uncertainty, even undecidedness, of the best educated of American presidents: Kennedy (Harvard), Carter (a nuclear engineer), Clinton (Oxford) and Obama (Harvard and Yale). Well, we can argue about Clinton, but he was decidedly uncertain in his first years. Knowledge makes one hesitate.

The second is from my apolitical friend Waleed Aly, who writes:

> Just as the public is disillusioned with politics in part because of the way politicians have devalued their field by attacking each other so relentlessly, so too is our predicament partly in our hands. What if, in the endless competition among ourselves, we're driving each other to do anything for a commercial advantage? What if our rivalries are driving us ever further into the profitable world of clickbait? Is it possible we'd be pursuing short-term victories at a more long-term cost to our authority?

Could it be that our annoyance with politics as a bad sport, as a war game, will deprive us, implies Aly, both of our democratic rights and of a thoughtful media, which instead is transformed to the level of clickbait?

The third is by Alan Bennett, writing in *Untold Stories*, whose dad, a bit like Ronnie Barker, was a butcher, small businessman and voted Tory:

> Without ever having been particularly left-wing
> I am happy never to have trod that dreary safari

from left to right which generally comes with age, a trip writers in particular seem drawn to, Amis, Osborne, Larkin, Iris Murdoch all ending up at the spectrum's crusty and clichéd end.

If I haven't it's partly due to circumstances: there has been so little that has happened to England since the 1980s that I have been happy about or felt able to endorse. One has only had to stand still to become a radical.

This is a comment I wholeheartedly agree with.

Sunshine

In the midst of turmoil there remain great supporters and enhancers of science.

Cate Blanchett has always been keen on science and technology, and gave us a fabulous videoed tribute at *The Science Show*'s fortieth birthday celebrations. She used to be on the Trust of the Australian Museum in Sydney, our second oldest scientific institution (1827) after Sydney's Royal Botanic Gardens (1816). She would arrive from her home in Hunters Hill without fuss, dressed in everyday clothes, and contribute with searing intelligence and professionalism. As one of the directors of the Sydney Theatre Company she investigated the possibilities of solar power for its many buildings and had it installed, thus giving the company a modern sheen as well as saving it plenty in power bills.

One day in 2014, having had a major cancer operation, I was receiving chemotherapy for the first time at St Vincent's Hospital in Darlinghurst. But I never allow fatal diseases or hideous treatments to interfere with my arrangements. I had worked out that I'd finish by 5 p.m. at the latest, and so would be able to stroll down the hill and along William Street to arrive at the Australian Museum on time at 5.15 p.m. to launch Tim

Flannery's latest book. This was *The Mystery of the Venus Island Fetish*, a frolic, a roman à clef about the Australian Museum itself and an unlikely anthropologist who unwisely sent his beloved what he meant as a traditional South Pacific love token: his dried and specially mounted foreskin. The romance did not go well.

I arrived on time at the museum with bandages on my left arm where the cannula had gone in and a somewhat disconnected brain. Otherwise I seemed OK. Then someone kindly gave me a glass of champagne. I'd received lots of instructions at the hospital about dealing with chemo, too many to take in, and one of them may have been a warning regarding drinking cold liquids. I suspect few of their patients would be likely to go from first infusion to a drinks party, so the nurses may not have emphasised the perils of chilled piss.

When I swallowed the champers a psychedelic explosion took place in my head. It was like a skull full of fireworks. What to do with a 15-minute speech on surreal anthropological fiction in front of me? I took another sip. A pink star whooshed through my head with descending blue sparkles. Try thinking? Pointless. I saw the people around me as in a dream, in that moment when you begin to come awake and figures float before settling as solid objects.

At this grim stage with minutes to go I spotted Cate Blanchett with her family, her husband, Andrew Upton, and their boys. She knew from Tim Flannery that I'd just had chemo and saw I was at a loss. You can't see inside someone's brain, fireworks or no, yet a well-practised thespian can tell if you are slightly off with the fairies. In theatre you need to be able to read other people whatever the barriers. She gave me a huge hug, a kiss and said encouraging things — just as I was being introduced in this long skeleton hall full of people.

It worked. I can't remember what I said through the pink fog but everyone seemed pleased. Tim Flannery then told them all about my cancer cure, if such it was, and we carried on. Cate's support had given me that sufficient human jolt to get me past mental collapse. Saved.

Tim is a superb writer and is often in the hallowed pages of *The New York Review of Books*. His first degree, in Melbourne, was in arts and it shows. I met him first at the Australian Museum in the 1980s when he was appointed as a mammalogist. His book *The Future Eaters* was the first step on the way to world fame and was a natural entry to his subsequent passion for climate science. Understanding the evolution of animal and plant life in Australia required a firm understanding of our Southern Oscillation, the way warmth in the Pacific Ocean is stored and leads to El Niño followed by La Niña events. That leads directly to comprehending how increasing heat will spoil the balance and cause extremes, big droughts, big floods and, well, future eating. Tim has been solid intellectually in following up the logic of this science and speaking publicly about what it means, often in the face of grotesque attacks from a vicious sector of the press.

Cate Blanchett has supported him throughout. One of the first times I met her was through Jeremy Leggett, the sun king. Jeremy used to be a geologist working for the fossil fuel industry. His own experience of the industry and its scientific implications made him leave oil and shift to solar. He runs one of the top companies in Europe in this field: Solar Century. Its commitment is to support the development of small, very cheap lighting devices to replace the noxious kerosene lamps used in Africa, South America and Asia. The kero gas kills over 3 million people a year and is a greenhouse disaster. The solar lamps sell for about $6 a pop and can be the basis for a village industry, enabling kids to do homework and keep their small homes free of fumes. Solar stoves are the next challenge.

The charity doing this, taking 10 per cent of Solar Century's profits, is called Solar Aid. Cate Blanchett was their first patron. Jeremy, on a visit to Australia, asked me to convene a dinner at Tetsuya's restaurant, hosted by Cate, at which our leading green-minded entrepreneurs could be told about the work.

I was impressed by how few leading Australians said no to dinner with Cate Blanchett at one of the world's top diners. Only one declined — and he was overseas. On the night I greeted her as 'Mrs Upton'. She was wryly amused. Her commitment to the solar story was knowledgeable and longsighted. It was a successful evening.

Attacks on Cate (and on Tim Flannery) in the hate press are both predictable and unwarranted. Australia has the good fortune to have many artists of the highest calibre. It is even more impressive that many of them stand for something that matters.

The lefty slur

As politics has become the snide exchange of slogans, so ideas have been devalued. Since when have wind turbines and solar technology been left? Why is climate science socialist, for God's sake? Why is coal (my father's deadly crystal) right wing?

'Lefty' has become a term of abuse, a slur employed to confuse the public — and confused we are, in this post-factual society. Mount a solid argument based on science, technology, economics — dare I say, philosophy — and all your opponent has to offer in reply is 'I am not convinced' or 'That's left wing' or 'You're part of the inner-city elite' or some reference to coffee. I don't even know what a latte is — am I missing something?

Yet in 2018 it is more than a hundred years since the Russian Revolution and the Bolsheviks (the original lefties) and 29 years since the fall of the Berlin Wall in 1989. 'Lefty' has become a lazy smear, strangely old-fashioned in this post–Cold War world.

If you want to say someone who believes in a civil society, is rather fond of the Australian egalitarian tradition that gave, for example, early votes to women beaten only by NZ — then yes, I am left. But that definition also includes most of the Tories I know. If it means wanting there to be a balance between funding those parts of society often neglected by the market (you know what they are) and simultaneously wanting enterprise to be vigorous, yet uncorrupted, then that's hardly being a raving lefty, more like a good soggy sensible Aussie in the Middle.

If I assembled all the leftist revolutionaries and pinko bomb throwers in Australia (or indeed America) outside Flinders Street Station they'd barely form a soccer team, let alone a mob. In a Fairfax article, Jonathan Holmes has affirmed, to our surprise, that ABC presenters 'undeniably' lean more to the left than the right. Yes, Jonathan, but then, so do you, and most tertiary-educated folk one comes across. This does not constitute a conspiracy. It constitutes a cultural mix and intellectuals (don't panic — I mean those who work with their minds) more commonly sound like reds than do manual workers. It used to be the other way around. Ask Gwyn Williams.

*

My father, Gwyn, was a left-winger from Central Casting. He went down the pit at the age of 14 and studied higher mathematics until nearly midnight every night despite his 4 a.m. start digging coal. He sang in the choir as a lyrical tenor, played rugby (a working-class religion in Wales), was as handsome as Gregory Peck in *To Kill a Mockingbird* — and became a Marxist when barely a youth after being converted by Uncle Ivor. Or was it Uncle Gareth? All Welsh uncles were Marxists then. Everyone is now dead so there's no way of checking.

Gwyn was born in 1905 and graduated as a mining engineer, so legend has it, coming first out of 2000 at Cardiff University at the age of 17 (just in time for the Great Depression). He would tell me this often to remind me of my incompetence. When doing maths or physics homework I would sometimes quote an imposs- ible question to him to reinforce the absurdity of what I was being asked to do and he would give me the answer immediately without taking breath. He was always right. I found this hopelessly intimidating.

Being left wing nearly broke him. After parading his degree up and down the Rhondda Valley and showing how dangerous the pits were, Gwyn was banned from the coalfields and had to go to London to get a job. He ended up on the buses. Being left in those days was a straightforward choice. Everyone who came out of the Great War was scarred, many families were in ruins and soon, so was Wall Street and the world economy. And another world war was but a blink away. In all the agony and strife you were either left or right, there was no in between — and right often meant fascism. My father chose; it was easy. Go left. Hitler's pact with Stalin seemed not to put him off.

One aspect of Gwyn puzzled me, but only in retro- spect. He had high-born friends. One of his closest was the nephew of Lord Craigavon, a delightful archi- tect with a social conscience who had been educated at Charterhouse and Trinity College, Cambridge, and served as a captain in the army (Guards, of course). They went to 'rugger matches' together and drank swank grog. Nares Craig was a friend of Virginia Woolf, HG Wells and Paul Robeson and I often wondered which of these Gwyn had met. I was also intrigued by the name Nares. Only the upper classes would call their son after a nostril. The man himself was wonderful in every way and applied his leftist beliefs to saving lives where it mattered by designing shelters that could be deployed in disaster zones following earthquakes and the like. His work made a real difference. When he and his Welsh wife Thora dropped around to our house in Sydney years ago, my children, then young teenagers, were at first sullen and unresponsive to these Oldies. However, when Nares started talking about homes for refugees, made cheaply but well, Tom and Jess were mesmerised. This was not empty talk from posh Pommies.

As I mentioned, after the war we went to Vienna where my parents (Mum was a lefty too) worked in a palace with marble staircases and chandeliers. Ray was a translator, specialising in German, Gwyn a union executive and occasional spy. We lived in the Russian Zone in a top flat with two servants (glorified nannies) and enjoyed the semi-diplomatic privilege and sumptuous living. But I was already beginning to perceive the tedium and legalistic tyranny of being a comrade in a bureaucratic setting: the unending meetings, the insufferable pecking orders, the false bonhomie. (David Aaronovitch of *The Times* in London has written of similar experiences in his 2016 book *Party Animals: My Family and Other Communists*.)

In 1955, we were kicked out of Vienna. I was told later that Gwyn had been too critical of Stalin's ruthlessness (the Welsh aren't very correct-line) despite

Uncle Joe having died two years before. You still had to toe the line about him, it seemed to me, until Nikita Khrushchev blew the whistle. We returned to London to a house my parents bought for $6000 (£2500) with a mortgage they found terrifying. (That same house, on Clapham Common West Side, was up for sale in 2016 for $7.5 million [£3.75 million].) Anthony Eden was prime minister, followed quickly by Harold Macmillan. Super-Mac epitomised upper-class Toryism and its essentially static policies. When, famously, he was asked what determined his decision-making, he replied, 'Events, dear boy, events.' You reacted to what happened; you didn't do anything so bolshie as *plan*. As for Five Year Plans — God forbid.

By 1955 Gwyn had become virtually unemployable. He ended up on street corners still loyally selling the *Soviet Weekly*. Our only perks were the occasional freebies for the Bolshoi Ballet and the Red Army Choir. His health had been ruined by foul food, the pit and too many unfiltered fags, but essentially he died, in 1962 at age 57, of a broken heart.

Despite his romantic vision of socialism, in the end he still defended the indefensible.

I had been a 1950s ban-the-bomb marcher, and he agreed that the British nuclear weaponry should go 'but not the socialist alternative'. Red bombs were good, blue bombs were bad. He was all for Stalin's nukes and tried to rise from his sickbed to argue the case. I was quietly incredulous. It was the day I gave ideology an almighty boot.

Marching for science

Both science and journalism are a search for truth. Science requires evidence from all over. Big numbers count. But so does *consilience*. In the 1830s the Master of Trinity College, Cambridge, Dr William Whewell, coined 'consilience' to mean many strands of evidence from different sources adding together to give confidence that something is so. Science does not triumph by plebiscite but through a *variety* of evidence. The same could be said of journalism: we need many sources to be confident that a case is made, a story is sound. Such meticulous discrimination, if applied conscientiously, makes bias difficult. Yet scientists and journalists (especially ABC ones) are often smeared with having left-wing inclinations.

We possess a vast capacity almost to work miracles to deal with the immense and urgent challenges facing our world — population growth, poverty, climate change, pollution and waste on a scale that may be unprecedented — yet we have a new politics combined with a newer media that too often prefers to undermine the science that can help us achieve those miracles.

In April 2017 around the world scientists and friends marched in protest, and to celebrate the worth of R&D.

In both Boston, Massachusetts, and Martin Place in Sydney, people spoke from the heart about what we stood to lose by sidelining science. In Boston it was Harvard professors such as Naomi Oreskes and researchers who'd never said boo before in public, let alone in the street, in front of thousands. In Sydney it was Simon Chapman, Professor of Public Health at Sydney University, John Hewson, former leader of the Liberals, and ... Jonica, who spoke simply and evocatively to a cheering crowd about what science gave her in the first ten minutes of every day: her phone-alarm clock, her clothing of man-made fibres, her breakfast of synthesised Vegemite and her electronic radio news. Then she mentioned climate.

We seemed to be defending the obvious. Should we have to?

*

Ahead of the march I had been in Boston in February to cover demonstrations put on to coincide with the annual American Association for the Advancement of Science (AAAS) meeting I always attend. I walked from my hotel to the large square where a protest was to start. Boston in winter can be bitingly cold and I was wearing a thin jacket. But today the sun was kind, taking away any chill and giving the gathering a real sense of occasion. There was snow on the footpath and lots of it swept, grey and sloshy, in the gutters, but when I came to it, the square itself, bounded by a cathedral and civic buildings of good age and dignity, had festive white patches over its green grass.

In the centre of the square scientists had already gathered, some in white coats, feeling they should look the part. A few had placards with polite messages and quite a few children were there with their parents, looking puzzled. Mummy and Daddy are not, they seemed to be thinking, the demonstrating type.

This was borne out when I took out my recorder and asked whether it was OK to put some questions for ABC Radio. Everyone agreed, but they all said that it was their first public demonstration; only a few feminists said they had also hit the streets once before in aid of causes for women. Some were professors at MIT and Harvard, a few were senior students doing PhDs, some were from other nations far away. All were disgusted by the actions of Trump barely a few weeks before, after he had taken office. They cited restrictions on the movement of foreign researchers, many already blocked from taking up or resuming their jobs in the USA; they cited promised cuts to research funding; they mentioned the threat of delayed appointments of senior administration staff in science and the massive disruption this would cause. Above all they were shocked by the proud, raucous anti-intellectualism of the new regime and its rhetoric against this public good, this search for knowledge.

A woman with a megaphone told us speeches would soon begin and they would come from those in different fields and from various parts of America to explain their distress and what could be done to reach citizens. She asked those who were *not* scientists to raise their hands to show that the demo was not simply an expression of self-interest. Many hands shot up. I asked a few for comments. They were articulate and moving — as you would expect in this world centre of academic excellence. But I asked myself, as Richard Nixon once did: 'How will this play in Peoria, Illinois?' How might it look in Struggle Street?

Then Professor Naomi Oreskes of Harvard spoke, in her slightly scratchy but compelling tones, explaining why so many paleo-conservatives assume scientists are merely on a lifelong diet of taxpayer funds and are therefore a branch of the dreaded government, which they always see as a pejorative term, and how so much of scientists' green findings also feed the kind of bad news that leads to more regulation and, eventually, world government. This had been a theme of her famous book *Merchants of Doubt*. I was reminded of the arguments I had sometimes had with government ministers in Sydney when I was president of the Australian Museum Trust. 'Another junket to Hawaii for one of your scientists,' accused Peter Collins when he was required to give ministerial approval for a trip. 'Yes, minister,' I replied, not for the first time, 'but you will find that the expenses are funded by an overseas grant that represents some 60 per cent of the funding we get from outside sources. It won't cost the taxpayer a bean.' He signed. (Naomi Oreskes, by the way, was originally trained as a geologist and worked in South Australia for three years for Western Mining. Never assume.)

I left the polite protest early as I wanted to cover a meeting back in the hotel where the AAAS had convened a number of groups to hear national leaders such as Professor John Holdren and Dr Jane Lubchenco, both

of whom had headed science for the Obama administration. I ran back, slipping on the ice, and found a hall
packed with people young and old and a fair display of
political banners — which would draw concerns from
the majority. I found the AV man and was distressed to
discover that there was no means to plug in a recorder.
So, I went to the front and stretched up to one of the
two loudspeakers and tested it for what is often a buzz,
making any recording un-broadcastable. It seemed OK
and, as the forum kicked off, I held my ancient mike
aloft and kept that position for the next hour and a half,
looking, as my arm ached, like a radio version of the
Statue of Liberty.

Holdren and Lubchenco spoke strongly. Any
decorum and reserve left over from high office was shed
and they explained, bluntly, why protest was now the
only recourse, but that it had to be from the community,
recognising how science improves our lives, not just from
academics apparently defending their careers. We were
also warned about the way public action can provide an
entry point for fellow travellers and malignant opportun-
ists. Some speakers even warned against demonstrations
because there would be those red or green flags waving
alongside earnest professors, confusing the message and
the multitude.

But what we heard from Holdren and Lubchenco
was primarily concern for the public interest, for being
aware of others' needs, for enlightenment. Both showed
why science is an international human activity like no
other, a culture of cooperation and of truth. There may
be villains (oh yes, even in science) but they get found out

and dealt with more quickly. This is why I put up with 90 minutes of throbbing arm ache, holding my mike aloft.

Here is some of what John Holdren said:

> So my advice to scientists, engineers, mathematicians, inside and outside of government, is as follows. First, don't be discouraged or intimidated. Second, keep doing your science, keep communicating about your findings and about their implications. Third, besides your own science, become more broadly informed about science and society issues. Fourth, get better at telling stories about how and why science matters and about how science works, and tell those stories to every audience you can find. Fifth, tie at least 10 per cent of your time to public service, including public and policy maker education and political engagement. And six, in that political engagement let us all be strategic. Let us recognise that we need better communication and coordination across all of the organisations that do this public-spirited work.
>
> If we let a thousand flowers bloom, which may well happen, one liability is that we will end up with a whole less than the sum of the parts. I think we need to be strategic across the AAAS, the academies, the university community, to figure out collectively where the leverage is and how to accomplish a division of labour and a degree of concerted and coordinated focus that gives us a whole more impactful than the sum of a thousand separate parts.

And Jane Lubchenco:

My advice first would be please don't make science partisan. It isn't, it shouldn't be, and don't buy into that framing. Secondly, I think we need to do a much better job of demonstrating, not just asserting, the relevance and importance of science. We know that it's important, but not everybody else does, and it's not enough to just say 'trust me, I know'. We need to do a better job in multiple ways of showing why it is relevant, showing why it's important, showing what it does for people.

Thirdly, much of science, especially in the world that I live in, which is environmental science, is often thought of as very doom and gloom science. And the reality is that there are some huge challenges facing the world. But it's also true that there is a wealth of really amazing solutions that are bubbling up all over the world, and we don't do a good enough job of telling the story about those solutions. They are not at the scale that they need to be, so we need to figure out how to replicate and scale those solutions. But giving people a sense of not just urgency but hope, and hope because people can work together, because science can help devise new solutions, is part of the message that I think we need to have.

Fourth, I would suggest that for those of us who live in the academic world, we need to pay a little more attention to our structures and reward systems in academia, and change the culture of academia so that it is more valued and rewarded for scientists to be engaged with society.

And fifth and finally I think it's really important for scientists to be more engaged with society, not just communicating science but working with communities, working with businesses, working with citizens through, for example, citizen science, but also information exchange in two ways. And I would assert that there are really exciting opportunities for scientists to get new ideas about research and to contribute immediately doing use-inspired science. So, there are some huge opportunities. And part of the reason that we are in the pickle that we are is that not enough people really appreciate and value science, and I think that's partly on us to help fix. So, I would suggest that now is a good time to take heart. This is actually not only an important but a really interesting and exciting time to be in science. We need to embrace these challenges and we need to be smart about it. I think now is the time for a quantum leap into relevance.

Jane was head of NOAA, the National Oceanic and Atmospheric Administration and is now back as a professor of marine science in Oregon. John is back at Harvard as a professor specialising in energy and policy. Compare their attitude to public service to that of their new (tax-payer funded) President, who has not bothered to fill their positions: he has no chief scientific adviser, nor the four deputies under the chief. The head of

NOAA is now not a scientist but a lawyer. Trump's contempt for science is not even disguised.

Nor, it has turned out, is that of the New South Wales Minister for Education Rob Stokes. He was on the front page of the *Sydney Morning Herald* in late March 2018 asserting that STEM (the acronym for Science, Technology, Engineering and Mathematics) is 'intellectual snobbery'. He went on: 'Ultimately, STEM seeks to dehumanise education — reducing it to an equation of inputs and outputs.'

The March for Science around the world took place on 22 April 2017. It was held in 58 countries. I marched in Sydney; there were 2000 to 3000 people with us and the good humour and remarkable lack of rancour was extraordinary. Since then, all has gone quiet. Scientists are not street-fighting men and women and they are quietly getting on with life as John and Jane in Boston suggested.

It is interesting, incidentally, that many in Australia had profound reservations about a march and spoke against it. One was Joan Leach, professor at the Centre for the Public Awareness of Science at the ANU. The academies were also chary, but did not advise against participating. Since April Australian researchers have, like their American colleagues, stayed in their labs.

I find their patience almost beyond belief. Look at the disruption occurring to their careers and projects. To PhDs, for example, and post-graduates. In November the journal *Nature* noted that 'From 2011 to 2012, more than half of [US] graduate students make less than US$20 000 a year. For reference, the federal poverty line for a single person without children is US$12 060.' And this is *before* the Trump tax cuts for higher income people make the situation even worse for those who have studied and toiled more than half their young lives.

In Australia the situation is barely much better. The rhetoric is fine, and I heard some superb unscripted orations from both former Minister Sinodinos and Opposition Leader Bill Shorten a year ago in federal parliament. But what does the real support look like?

In late 2017 I broadcast a talk by Professor Norman Saunders about the plight of PhDs in medical lines in Australia. It turns out that barely half stay in science on becoming 'doctored'. As for investment in an area we are supposed to perform well in, he says:

> Many will argue that the problem can be fixed by greater funding of research by government. In this regard Australia's record is pitiful, especially given that we are a rich country. A common way of defining research investment is expressing it as a percentage of Gross Domestic Product, known as GDP. Australia is well towards the bottom of the league table of OECD countries in expending 0.4 per cent GDP. Only Slovakia and Spain are worse. The figure for the UK is 0.57 per cent and for the US nearly twice Australia's at 0.75 per cent. Many EU countries approach or are above 1 per cent GDP.
>
> Since 2013–14 the NHMRC [National Health and Medical Research Council] budget has fallen by about 4 per cent and ARC [Australian Research

Council] by 14 per cent and this does not take
account of increases in wage and salary costs, the
latter is often much greater than the general level of
inflation.

Leigh Dayton, a friend of mine who once reported
science for Fairfax and then *The Australian* newspaper,
has now herself completed a PhD on innovation and how
we performed in 2016. In the Global Innovation Index,
she writes, we came ninth for 'Input' (the smart research
upon which development is based); 27th for 'Output'
(innovations); and 73rd for the 'Efficiency' (collaboration between campus and industry). In the OECD itself,
for this metric, we came last out of 21 countries.

When the PM, Malcolm Turnbull, reshuffled his
cabinet before Christmas 2017 he replaced the ailing
Sinodinos with Michaelia Cash, a lawyer, in the port-
folio of Jobs and Innovation. Science was an add-on.
The president of Science and Technology Australia (the
peak body), Professor Emma Johnston, said: 'This is the
fourth minister we've had in three years, and the second
time that we have not had a federal Minister for Science
— if science is not a priority, we risk damaging the sector
and Australia's future health, wealth and wellbeing'.

The day before the universities' funding was effectively cut by nearly $3 billion and regional campuses
were placed especially at risk.

Get the trend? Scientists should march every day,
I'd have thought, and not be so shy about upsetting
the Neanderthals — or even those blue collars who
now favour UKIP, One Nation or the Donald. It is

about time both realised just how much wealth comes from R&D and how much faster it should emerge. According to Emma Johnston, for every $1 invested by the National Health and Medical Research Council, $3.20 is returned. 'In Europe,' she writes, 'science provides a 250 per cent return on investment.' The figures for USA and the UK match those of Europe.

As Jonica put it in her speech in Martin Place, science affects our lives every minute of every day, usually in a positive way. It does so for all people, deplorables like me, or otherwise. That we have leaders who fail to comprehend this is one of the twenty-first century's greatest tragedies. It could kill us.

Australian science stars

Now let's do a thought experiment about the Lucky Country and how aware it is of the scientific stars we have, and have had, in our midst.

Question 1: Who invented a new branch of science while working in an old shed once used for spotting enemy aircraft? It was a few hundred metres from Bondi Beach, up on Dover Heights. He found an ex-galactic star and thus pioneered radio astronomy. He was recruited to build dishes at the renowned Caltech (California Institute of Technology) in Pasadena, refused to stay in a highly prestigious professorship in the USA but instead came back to run a telescope built in a sheep paddock. He should have won a Nobel Prize but there wasn't one for astronomy at that time. He was played in the movie by Sam Neill.

Answer: Dr John Bolton, who set up and ran the Dish at Parkes. It brought you the walk on the moon in 1969. The secret: a bunch of smart people who'd come together to develop radar during World War II and gone on to apply their knowledge in a brand-new field with good leadership and proper resources. Most of them were engineers with bugger-all knowledge of astronomy, which they taught themselves as they went along.

There is a memorial up on Dover Heights to mark the breakthrough.

It is an interesting paradox that the Other John Bolton, once mouthing fire and fury at the United Nations as George W Bush's ambassador, is now back as President Trump's Security Adviser. Could there be such a contrast between the quiet, super-achieving scientist and the intemperate, pugnacious wrecker? Fiona Wood versus Rosa Klebb, perhaps?

Question 2: Who was born in Hobart, did her science in Melbourne, and won the Nobel Prize for Medicine in 2009? She was recruited to serve as a senior adviser to the US government, refused to bend to the preposterous requirements of President George W Bush and said so boldly. She is now president of the renowned Salk Institute. She was secretly invited to become the first woman in history to lead the Royal Society in London in the footsteps of Newton and Florey. She said no, wanting to keep doing research in San Francisco.

Answer: Professor Elizabeth Blackburn. Her work on telomeres, which cap DNA molecules, and the enzyme telomerase, which regulates their activity, could revolutionise how we handle ageing and the diseases thereof. She was nurtured by the magnificent critical mass of excellence in immunology and related research in Melbourne.

Question 3: Who did his latest research at age 92 (he is now 94), linking drug addiction with the part of the brain controlling salt and thirst? He was the founding director of the Florey Institute and married to the woman who set up the Australian Ballet School (and danced in

The Nutcracker Suite at the age of 69, her artificial hip notwithstanding). Both have the highest Australian award: the AC.

Answer: Professor Derek Denton and Dame Maggie Scott (whose former student Graeme Murphy choreographed *The Nutcracker* for his teacher). Denton is a model of someone building international networks (and funding) to support Australian research. As a couple they represent STEAM — something all should applaud and support: STEM + Arts.

Question 4: Who came to Australia because our reputation in physics rivalled that of Harvard, applied to the ANU three times and was turned down? He eventually got in to continue his work on cosmology, matched this with oenology, and now grows some of the best pinot noir in Australia?

Answer: Professor Brian Schmidt, Nobel laureate in physics and vice-chancellor of the ANU. Secret: persist.

Question 5: Who was born in Adelaide a month before I started *The Science Show* and is now, aged 42, considered to be one of the top mathematicians in the known universe? He has won the Fields Medal (in 2006, always said to be equivalent to the Nobel Prize) and refuses to be interviewed because he'd rather be teaching his students and working on equations. He is now a professor at UCLA.

Answer: Professor Terence Tao. His wife, Laura, is a NASA engineer working at the Jet Propulsion Lab in Pasadena. I interviewed him at last in February 2018. He was a delight. I was surprised to learn that he did not know that the present president of the Royal Society of

London, in succession to the likes of Newton, Wren and Florey, had gone to Unley Primary School in the suburbs of Adelaide: Venki Ramakrishnan.

I could go on. We have the stars. Few are known. I am continually astonished by how little (and how proudly) many Australians deny much knowledge of their own scientific heritage. This is encouraged, as I have indicated, by tireless noise machines painting our academics as an 'elite' with no knowledge of those 'battlers'.

One excuse is the youth of our scientific establishment. The Australian Academy of Science is barely 60 years old. Before Sir Mac Burnet's example of doing most of his work at the bench in Australia, all of our top boffins like Florey and Oliphant went OS and stayed there until they were grey. And, as the example of John Bolton illustrates, in the old days, up to when I began to broadcast, scientists in Australia were discouraged from going public. It was considered infra dig and some outfits, such as the CSIRO and Defence Science, forbad public exposure beyond carefully managed bland announcements. Nowadays the scene is so raucous it is hard to isolate what counts amid the cacophony.

Hence the march. Hence the need for politicians in Australia who commit to a knowledge of R&D. Who can you name after Barry Jones or Peter McGauran (yes, he tried and did well) who were effective ministers of science? How many retain their understanding of its importance over our absurd three-year electoral cycle and the rapid extinction of prime ministers? How can long-term science policy survive the modern Australian habit of firing most of the top public servants with their deep knowledge of their subjects at every change of government, in favour of compliant cronies? It kills corporate memory and nous. It doesn't work now in the USA either. I was not surprised to read that, at the time of the invasion of Iraq by the Willing nations (the USA, UK, et al.) there were only eight speakers of Arabic in the State Department. No wonder the event was a shambles.

New Zealand, again, is an example of what can be done. The Kiwis have some of the best universities in the world and even a space industry (until recently Australia was the last OECD country without a nationally led industry, alongside Iceland). I am often reminded of the contrast between our two nations in the form of favourite comedy geniuses: Barry Humphries and John Clarke. They share a love of language and a fondness for culture and excellence in art (Humphries, painting; Clarke, wildlife photography) and history. The difference: cruelty.

Barry Humphries' fun is utterly cruel. I have been at his theatrical performances on many a night and been hugely relieved I was not in the front rows. It was clever, certainly, but without a smidge of pity or humility. Just like a querulous youth, his comedy is essentially puerile, snarling schadenfreude. Kiwi John Clarke was the opposite. If he satirised bad behaviour, it was to condemn it. But Clarke was invariably a jolly conjurer with brilliant language and portraiture. His lumpen figures are fun, not grotesque. He was adult, in the best way, like his former home.

We have, in Australia, wonderful patches of magnificence. We also have blights of mediocrity. In 1960

Robin Boyd published a book about architecture called *The Australian Ugliness*. I was surprised to find when I heard it discussed, that many took the slur as a compliment. The same occurred when Donald Horne's book came out 50 years ago.

I think we need more marches for science. And culture.

Denialism

Ian Plimer was on the staff of Newcastle University, north of Sydney, when I first met him. He was young and good looking at that stage, already with white hair, but not quite as well lunched as he looks today. His expertise, matching that of Jeremy Leggett way back when, was in mining geology. This was in the mid-1980s. Thereafter he moved to the University of Melbourne, then Adelaide.

Our first collaborations on radio were about rocks and about religion. He showed a vigorous scepticism when it came to God's role in Creation. In 1997 he took on Allen Roberts of the Hills Bible Church who'd claimed to have found evidence of Noah's Ark up a mountain in Turkey. Plimer chose to use the *Trade Practices Act* to sue, implying that Roberts was using false advertising to promote his idea. In the essentials of the case Plimer won, but the trouble was that the judge, having agreed that the ark was not likely to be Noah's, nonetheless awarded expenses against our smooth geologist on the basis that the case did not fit the Act's intention. Costs were about $1 million and so Plimer had to sell his house to pay them.

The professor of geology seemed surprisingly sanguine at the time, saying, 'The Lord giveth and the Lord taketh away', but this may have been the experience that tipped him over the edge. We gave him Eureka Prizes to recognise his fortitude against the Forces of Darkness, but a few of us began to think he had, in fact, joined them. The event that drew the line for me was a speech he gave (several times) on the Bible's version of world history. It was amusing in parts but in others veered towards rant and insult. As an atheist, I am willing to engage in all kinds of robust exchanges on God and the meaning of life, but I will not insult someone's spiritual beliefs nor treat them with contempt personally — unless they are doing wilful harm with, for instance, female genital mutilation or similar subjugation of an individual in the name of the Almighty. But Plimer was not being so discriminating. Anything pious was fair game. And the language was blokey and loud. (This, in the end, became the problem with dear old departed Bill Leak and much of the commentary columns in *The Australian* newspaper. Not a question of non-PC but of an endless narky tone. Not funny, just bilious.)

I felt our 'hero' was going too far.

Then came climate. There are three kinds of 'climate denier'. There are those who simply won't contemplate the evidence because it is an inconvenient truth — too inconvenient for their casual value systems as lay people, so it's dismissed. Then there are those Tom Griffiths, the distinguished historian at ANU, describes as either natural contrarians or suffering from attention deprivation disorder in later life. Plimer may be both of these, but he is also much more. I indicated earlier that you get a certain pattern of behaviour if you line up USA presidents such as Nixon, Reagan, Bush 1 and 2, and Trump. There is a ruthless and unswerving ideology among all of them, untainted by erudition. This is the third kind of 'denying'. Trump claims never to have had time to read a book in his life, and he behaves accordingly. It is power that matters, not learning or subtlety. Plimer has an encyclical on climate change that I have heard many times. I begged him to vary it when once more I agreed to broadcast his views. I say this to everyone I broadcast on any subject — please don't say exactly the same as you did last time, for the sake of the listener — but no, *here it comes again*. Unblushingly. I could lip-sync every word.

Tom Griffiths has written about 'why an admired scientist turns on his peers and professional culture'. His essay on denialism was reproduced in *Best Australian Science Writing 2014*:

> This move from defending the scientific method
> to fighting climate science seems dramatically
> contradictory. But Plimer would presumably argue
> for continuity between his two campaigns, one to
> expose 'fraudulent creation science' and the other
> to reveal that the IPCC [Intergovernmental Panel
> on Climate Change] is 'underpinned by fraud'. He
> would also see himself defending science against two
> evangelical positions. But his lone, zealous advocacy
> against the scientific community now seems very
> like the creationism he reviled years earlier.

His language carries no restraint. A Plimer article (the cover story in *Spectator Australia*) was called 'Climate Crimes'. It contained the following:

> By denying poor countries access to fossil fuels, Pope Francis condemns them to permanent poverty with the associated disease, short life and unemployment. The Pope seems to have swallowed hook, line and sinker the new environmental religion that competes with Catholicism. His encyclical is an anti-development, anti-market enthusiastic embrace of green left environmental ideology … a denunciation of free-markets dressed up as religious instruction … We have been conned with a non-problem at huge expense to the taxpayer.

Climate a 'non-problem'? Seriously?

Plimer has scorched the sky with his travelling and had crates of his anti-climate books bought by mining corporations and handed out as gifts to mates at golf clubs. He has joined any number of boards of the rich and powerful. Good luck to him. But it is his debauching of climate science I've found to be unforgivable, ignoring as it does centuries of evidence, sophisticated investigation from innumerable *separate* sources — from chemistry, physics, biology, mathematical modelling and, indeed, geology, as well as astronomy (such as the history of carbon dioxide on Venus). Plimer refuses to engage doubt. He does not see that any force for change must involve a degree of risk. It may be slight, such as my next trip on a plane to America, but we all take this into account in the lives we lead. We insure. Nothing is 100 per cent or zero. Not in terms of risk. So what *is* the risk of climate change? For our families and for our nation we need to make a judgement. No true citizen will refuse this challenge. We do it for our health, our children's education, our economy. It's a necessary duty in life. I would aver that in 2018 the risk we face with climate is clearly dire.

Why is it that those who deny climate change will not engage in this simple exercise? Assess risk and behave accordingly. And why is it that they are uniformly on the far right of politics? Plimer is with Gina Rinehart and Margaret Thatcher's former treasurer Nigel Lawson on the Take No Prisoners side of politics.

But it is for his wilful attacks on top-line climate science that I proposed (as the person who helped invent the Eureka Prizes) that his 1995 prize for the promotion of science (!) be withdrawn. It is a mark of the politeness of the scientific community that they felt too chary to follow my entreaty. We may live to regret our caution.

The world is becoming a more uncertain place to live. Ian Plimer has done a great deal to make it worse.

Success or failure?

This book is about paradoxes. In a way it's about my life. I can be called a success; if you listen to the introductions as I go on stage for the thousandth time in some town hall or auditorium, I sound like a plausible achiever: I have broadcast high-rating programs on radio and TV in Australia and other countries for more than 40 years; I have an honours degree from the University of London and seven honorary doctorates; I have had two fellowships at Oxford and two professorships in Australia; I am a fellow of the Australian Academy of Science and former president of the Australian Museum; I have an Order of Australia and am a National Living Treasure; I am deputy chair of the Australian Science Media Centre and former chair of the Commission for the Future; I have a centenary medal from John Howard and was president of the Australian Science Communicators. I have a trophy wife, as her mother keeps reminding me; a treasured ex-wife, a flourishing son and daughter and five grandsons; I have no debts and my own home and no enemies of consequence. When in England I was in *Monty Python*, *Doctor Who* and *The Goodies* and played an apostle in Dennis Potter's play *Son of Man* (I was the one next to the camel) and met any number of Namedrops.

I have a star named after me. Apparently, I'm obliged to go there.

Look on my works, Ozymandias, and despair!

So where exactly is the problem? Why should I think I am a failure? Because you could also pull the switch and make a convincing case that I've stuffed up wholesale. Stay in the ABC too long and you absorb the sense of doom — like a new Oz PM on the way to Government House, constantly wondering 'How long will I survive?'

I once asked Jonica: 'I suppose you got a top first-class honours degree when you graduated in veterinary science in Perth?' Yes, she replied, but that was *only* because I memorised everything. *Only.*

'And I guess you fluked the top degree of the year too. How did you do with your high-school results? *Only* first or second in the state in most subjects?'

So it turned out, of course. Top or near top in every subject. And there was an excuse for each achievement, each record held: too few entrants, only a side subject, not the main topic, memory flukes again ... and so on it went. Why, I wondered, do men inflate their achievements and women invariably minimise theirs?

Yes, I have a degree from London University, but it was a pretty ordinary one, a gentleman's degree — but better than Christopher Hitchens'. I couldn't be bothered attending practical experiments on two tedious afternoons per week and, just like at school, thought I could revise the whole thing the night before exams and keep going without sleep for two weeks. I also spent half my time appearing as a human prop on television. Yes, I have seven doctorates, but if you live long enough most people in public life get lucky, they get doctored; matriculation is harder. I was a Reuters Fellow at Green College Oxford, but got in as the first candidate from the ABC, before they provided grants for Auntie's broadcasters, because Reuters wanted to get someone from Australia and I was handy and knew those in charge. And, yes, Balliol College is a wonderful place to spend a year but I just happened to know a few college members and they felt like having a rogue journalist there for a change instead of some dry don.

As for that brilliant career: yes, I have been in the ABC forever but science always strikes others as difficult so they'll readily let you have it to yourself as it is in the charter and so must be done. They have to put up with you. In radio if you work hard and cut out the mistakes you can sound OK and carry on forever. I tend to stay in a place for ages in whatever I do, so I can end up seeming essential (or just useful). And, in the 1970s when I wrote to those with whom I grew up in England about my career and all this public exposure, they responded in that characteristic Pommy way: 'Yes, well, fine, but it's *only* Australia, after all, isn't it?' You know the song, I sing it all the time: 'Always Look on the Shite Side of Life!'

And those various appointments, quangos and the like: one could say, peering on the down side as one must, looking for the worst, that, if you hang around in a field long enough, someone will eventually want to bung you on a committee. And National Living Treasure? Yes, sure, but remember Clive Palmer is one too.

As for those celebrated appearances with the Pythons and whomever: in those days, half a century ago, the programs were not of very much consequence and years away from cult status. They were more like undergrad frolics. Back then *Doctor Who* still had sets that wobbled and a cast that stood around shouting. I had a couple of minor agents who handled extras and small part *artistes*, and I simply turned up thrice a week in weird locations like abandoned factories or fallow fields, ran around as directed with little idea of the main plot — the studio recording came later. We found out what had been going on only if we happened to see the actual broadcast weeks afterwards when the bits had been assembled. The Pythons were rather reserved, donnish chaps, talking about making their lines 'sillier' rather than funnier, and could sound like older students at a tutorial on language. As for *Doctor Who*, I vaguely recall it may have been Patrick Troughton who was the Doctor at that time and we were in something like an underground car park dressed like security men in an extraterrestrial abattoir and just hung about looking glum and saying 'rhubarb' to each other. That had to be done without characterisation — hence 'rhubarb' instead of real dialogue — because pretending personality, really acting, cost extra according to Equity, the actors' union, and so we were discouraged unless we had a real part.

What about this long career I can look back on and prospects for the future? Surely a record of decades is unassailable? Well, 'experience' can nowadays be recast as just plain old. Being a veteran can always be seen as blocking the way for new talent and as someone whose abilities must soon fade. *Always look on the shite side of life ...*

Everyone, except for male sociopaths, feels that one day they'll be found out. Women seem to be different and apparently need to prompt you to find them out, so Jonica is not the only woman to diminish her talents and her record. I just wish she wouldn't do it so often. And while mentioning her I must admit that, in personal terms, I have indeed been lucky living with her for so long and so happily. It is well worth repeating.

Family and friends are also quite wonderful and I can't imagine having done better — but you never know what mishap is around the corner. The secret, oddly enough, of family and social success is the same as the rather dour ingredient of my professional existence: trying to be dependable. If you can't do brilliance, try graft. My father told me often that I would never match his flair with maths and analysis and I believed him. Even today if you give me a puzzle to solve I will go blank. I specialise in what's left, the stolid and reliable: the history of science, animals and science policy (which only wrinklies worry about), not maths and biochemistry. It is a prosaic choice requiring constant toil and the relentless meeting of deadlines. Stolidly. The mission statement: how can I be a rock (instead of a rock star)?

Men are to blame, of course. As I said, I learned this early on when my clever father told me at length how I could not do various tasks, from maths to DIY — at which he was magnificent. Accordingly, I assumed I would be hopeless. Was it because I was an unexpected child in an unplanned relationship (my parents had never married)? Was it because I did not look like him, but my (more favoured) brother did? I shall never know, as Gwyn died when I was 18. But I still recognise his legacy and expect the worst. I do not enter programs for awards — there's no point.

Real chaps can be convinced they are born to rule. It helps to send them to posh schools specialising in the elevation of self. Then it comes naturally.

I am also impressed again and again by how Masters of the Universe manage to gamble with the world's fortunes on stock exchanges, fuelled, as Cambridge research confirms, by overdoses of testosterone and a complete absence of self-doubt. It is a wonder that they and their ilk, having managed to give us the GFC in 2008 and bring ruin to most of the world, have themselves largely survived the experience, even managed to flourish and become as rich as before. Richer. How do they get away with it, those smooth, unbelievably narrow wonders? Those male caricatures?

*

Long ago Norman Swan told the *Sydney Morning Herald* that I resented powerful men. 'I think he suffered greatly from his father dying when he was relatively young,' Norman wrote. 'He clearly adored his father. It may be why he has an ambivalent attitude towards dominant male figures. He's attracted to strong powerful men, but if strong powerful men try to exert any control over him, he pushes back.'

I denied it, of course. But he was half right. I resent men without the redeeming qualities that a feminine side can give them. These fellows are always in a hurry, can't talk to you without scanning the periphery, inevitably have a phone to inspect while supposedly listening to you and can make ruthless decisions without a qualm. Does a word with *path* at the end of it occur to you? Caused perhaps by testosterone poisoning?

This is one reason I have always enjoyed the friendship and collegiality of gay people. I once wrote that there is evidence for a special creation by God, for Intelligent Design, but only *once* in the history of the world. You see He must have created homosexuals. They are, after all, unable to evolve (in theory) and adoption or IVF doesn't count. They won't, in the main, pass on their genes (possible now, just) and so must have been put here for a special purpose: to foster the essential ingredients of human culture. Just consider the names — Gertrude Stein, Leonardo da Vinci, kd lang, Stephen Fry, Bridget Kendall, Oscar Wilde, Sandi Toksvig, Alan Turing, Dusty Springfield, Graham Chapman, Noel Coward, Robyn Archer, Michelangelo, Miriam Margolyes, George Michael, Ellen DeGeneres, Alan Bennett, Michael Kirby, Penny Wong, Oliver Sacks, Ian McKellen, Kylie Kwong, Benjamin Britten, Sappho ...

Compare 'real men' in all their unstoppable masculinity: Mel Gibson, Tony Abbott, Gwyn Williams, Shane Warne, Bluto, Jeffrey Archer, Dick Cheney, Barnaby Joyce, John Wayne, Lenin, Iron Man ...

And then there are real men with a good amount of girl added: Phillip Adams, Tim Minchin, the late, divine John Clarke, Peter Garrett, Tony Jones, Ferdinand the Bull, B1 and B2, Barack Obama, AC Grayling, Paul McCartney, Ian McEwan, all the boys in my family ...

Try your own lists. Then see how easy it is to rede-fine your successes as pitiful fails.

*

My mother was a failure. She didn't start that way. As a teenager she was selected to represent England (or some part of it — the records have gone) in netball and trav-elled all over Europe, speaking several languages with ease and taking a job, after the war, as a high-level trans-lator in Vienna. She was attached, as was my father, to an international organisation and did well.

When we were evicted from Austria in 1955, Ray found a job as a PA in the Royal Automobile Club in St James, not far from Buckingham Palace. I pass it often when in London as I stay at the Royal Society, just around the corner from the RAC and Pall Mall.

One day, Ray collapsed. She was brought home an invalid, unable to leave the house for the next 25 years. Her nerves had gone and she was housebound with agoraphobia. She spent her time at the kitchen table with a kettle permanently on the stove popping and rumbling as she drank endless cups of tea and smoked cheap fags called Weights.

Her biggest worry, apart from the outside world in its entirety, was her house. She had never married Gwyn and had doubts about the ownership that gave her night-mares. I was in Australia by the time these worries got really bad and I returned to find her morose and dis-tracted. And that's when I reacted like a real man to solve her problem at a stroke.

I called one of my friends just qualified in law at Oxford. He'd put his shingle up in South London and was willing to do a favour. He sorted the probate, and therefore the ownership of the family house, in a couple of hours.

And my mother's reaction? Yes, relief. But also a tinge of humiliation. Years of anxiety and circular thoughts dismissed by a couple of young squirts as if it were all nothing. It took me a while to comprehend her mixed feelings.

But was she really a failure, notwithstanding her collapse and incarceration? (Is Jonica, evicted at a stroke from the ABC with all her colleagues? Am I?)

Not for a minute. Ray ruled from her kitchen chair as innumerable friends and family dropped in for a guaranteed cup of tea and whatever else was on offer from a generous but frugal cupboard. She relished gossip and argument and whatever human action came her way. In the meantime she read, devoured everything the BBC had to offer, and wrote to the prime minister about whatever outrage had inflamed her febrile sense of injustice that week, that minute. She lived in the moment.

Which is what we do. I have had, essentially, the same job since 1972. I have the personal ambition of a parrot, caring only about the next dish of seed, taste of nectar and the next frolic, be it another program to be made or another trip somewhere nice, as well as relishing every minute with something to read, something to discover. Jonica is the same: surfing, skiing, riding, running, dancing, eating chocolate, finding joy in chick lit as well as crit lit.

Both of us follow Flaubert, who understood the importance of a comfortable routine and predictability: 'Be regular and orderly in your life, so that you may be violent and original in your work.'

We shall never reach the top, if that's where 'success' resides, because we're having too much fun. And that's fine — as long as the chaps with the rule book and the control, the real men, don't stop the fun. It is they who create real failure. Look at the evidence: the turbulence of our difficult age.

Slum child

This is what Jonica sometimes calls me. In a way it's true. After my family's time in the lap of luxury in Vienna, we fell severely from grace in the 1950s.

Our family income back then was minuscule, and when my father died in 1962, virtually non-existent. There was no widow's pension for my mother — as an unmarried woman she wasn't a widow. She had a tiny sickness benefit and that was it. I did newspaper rounds, collected bottles to claim the deposits in the off-licence (grog shop) and we just went without. In the great British phrase that covered so many families during and after the war, we 'made do'.

It's a habit that stays with you. Here, in 2018 I own no car, have no mobile, have never owned a camera, golf clubs or similar kit; I live in a house called Termite Towers that is 3.6 metres wide and I haven't bought clothes in over a decade. As the ABC gets ever more austere, as they take away our offices and make us work in call centres, I react like Brer Rabbit 'born and bred in a briar patch': I make do among the nettles.

When I began *The Science Show* in 1975 we had producers attached, reporters on standby in various parts of the world and in parts of Australia, and I would commission what I thought could be good that week almost without limit. No longer. *The Science Show* team is now me and David Fisher. And we both do much more than that one show. There are no researchers, no reporters here or anywhere else. I rely on rule 17 subsection 34 of the Old Mates Act. If a friend has been sent somewhere by the BBC or some other broadcaster, I get offered a piece for me, on a freelance basis, of course. This makes it appear that I have reporters at my disposal, but I can't *ask* them to do anything unless they are already going somewhere anyway. So, you can't pick an important topic and ask a reporter to follow it up thoroughly as we once did. Then there are friends such as Sharon Carleton who are always willing to try a feature, if there's time, as a favour. We *make do*.

If I go on holiday, to Greece or Galapagos or even to Shoalhaven, I magically find a recorder with me and make shows for the ABC. And I also cut costs personally. It's another game.

So, sometimes, when off on my own for the weekend, if I find say $15 dollars in my pocket, I try to make it stretch out for all meals. Buy a bag of spuds from Paddy's Market, plus some mushrooms and a veg (Brussels sprouts) and three corn cobs for three lunches all for $5, two chicken drumsticks for 80 cents, and a loaf of bread on special ($4) and you're on your way. That'll last three days. (One caveat: there is always wine provided by the Bottle Fairy, but that would spoil the story, wouldn't it?) There is usually stuff lingering in the fridge left by other intemperate people — to hell with the use-by date. If it's not putrid or furry it's OK. *Slum child.*

Nothing gets thrown away if it is at all useful. The magazines we get sent have an address on one side of an A4 sheet inside the plastic bag. I turn the paper to its blank side, put it in my typewriter, and do my script. Yes, typewriter. That's what enables me to use no fresh paper supplies, as well as relying on the limitless sheets abandoned at every photocopier or printer by cavalier colleagues. I have not used a sheet of new paper since 1972. Does it make any difference to the world and our green future? Probably not. But I never have the impasse of computer failure or a printer jam — my scripts are always ready. At least until the typewriter ribbon eventually runs out one day. I have six left. (Stop press: the head of Radio National, Deb Leavitt, when passing through Amherst, Massachusetts, has found a typewriter shop stocking ribbons — I am extended for three years.)

There is a theory, augmented by experience, that governs my radio scripting. It matches the prohibitions on driving while talking on your mobile. Your attention is diminished on both. I write on the typewriter and play sound and edit on the computer. At the same time, but they are separate. It works. I often have kind remarks made about the precision of my scripts (do look up Les Murray's sweet poem on 'The Privacy of Typewriters') and I am often mystified by some awful writing, as Murray remarks, that must have looked so neat and credible on the screen.

People will tell you I don't use computers and combine this with the absence of a mobile to accuse me of being a Luddite. Not true. I'm not Ned Ludd and, besides, he never existed. I just hate waste and loathe unwanted communication. I do carry a phone made of wood and slate sent to me by Henry Hoke. It is the Hoke's phone and was sent to me by a prankster who made the ABC TV series *The Lost Tools of Henry Hoke*, about the inventing genius from Hoke's Bluff. (Remember? Written by the mischievous Mark Thomson, it was narrated by Bryan Dawe. Look it up online and weep with joy.) I often take it out and stride through hotel atria shouting instructions to my imaginary broker as I hold it to my ear. Or I do thumb dances on it at the table or when walking down the corridor. It has a stick of chalk inside and you can extract it, write a message on the slate and give it to your interlocutor to reply. Real men blink in confusion.

Ultimately my life will have made no difference to the rise or fall of civilisation, but aesthetically it is sublimely satisfying to use just what's needed and no more. It is also fun to tease the neophiliacs who insist on having each iGadget as it comes out of the iFactory whatever the vast iCost.

I use radio headphones bought from Radio Shack in the USA for $25. The plastic joins are falling apart so I fix them (as I do my trousers) with gaffer tape. Senior managers at the ABC are apoplectic about this and urge me to get a phone with an app — for a mere $900. An iDevice costing 36 times mine and with at least 15 capacities I don't need and wires dangling where now I have none.

What is the point of all this derro behaviour? Apart from efficiency, privacy and the chance to be smug, it allows me to be lavish when I need to be. If you don't spend like a normal chap on steroids, you can save masses. This is the lesson of the slum child. All those lunchtimes as a boy with nothing to eat, all those hitch-hiking holidays sleeping on beaches and watching the well-off swanning in and out of shining hotels. If you want to have what the rich have, spend nothing and hoard cash.

So it is that I now have June in Greece and the Amalfi Coast. We fly business. We have to. Jonica has a part-tungsten spine and can't sit in a seat for more than two hours, and I have no rectum. Cancer took that and half my gut in 2014. Try economy toilets with personal plumbing like that. Doesn't work. If the queue in economy is long, as it always is, I am in deep trouble. So are my trousers.

This means that, being in the twilight years with no mortgage and parsimonious habits of an almost clinical kind, I can wave a financial wand. I just unleash those savings and upgrade life aloft. People in the corporate world hearing this are incredulous. They really believe we exist only on the taxpayer's teat.

Yours truly, the Luddite derelict, is also able to wave a magic family wand when emergencies occur, unlike my own parents who ended up with no such choices.

Does it take some kind of partially crippled mind, the psyche of the hopelessly anal retentive, to live like this? Am I utterly OCD? Well, you do notice too much real life if you are me: how others throw away too much, how they observe use-by dates to the minute, buy too much, squander. When I line up at supermarkets and see trolleys piled high as if to feed and wipe an army,

I want to unload nearly all of it and then confiscate their dozens of plastic bags. Aren't they *thinking*? Those over-large damp blokes with huge bellies and big shorts and larger ladies who always pay with plastic cards and take forever to enter their numbers. Oh, the self-righteous frustration! 'You can't possibly eat all those grey sausage rolls! Why d'you need 50 bottles of Virgin Spring Water imported from distant alps, you're not in the Simpson Desert! Is your cuisine made up entirely of diet boxes of gluten-free frozen crap?'

Jonica prefers not to go shopping with me. I carry a cloth bag I acquired in 1996 to buy three small items, all on special. She does want me to go to a good shop with her to buy clothes but I reply I did that also in 1996 and what with the odd shirt provided as a Christmas present I've calculated that I now have more apparel than I have likely lifespan. *Derro.*

But it is instructive to do calculations on those energy bills people are cross about and which seem to be influencing elections. Why don't folk turn things off? I can find about a third of the devices in a house or an office switched on unnecessarily. People don't notice. Maybe they don't care, despite whingeing about the hefty bills.

*

This training in the slums does, however, mesh nicely with environmental sensitivity. It is crazy to throw away so much of Australia's food: about 30 to 40 per cent per annum or $25 billion worth. At least. There's nothing more sickening than seeing a party with catering for at least twice the number of people present — not that fewer have turned up, just that so much more grub is provided than was remotely sensible. It is inelegant. Good food is invariably dumped for 'health' reasons.

As for the rest: paper lasts for two to five months on a tip; plastic-coated milk cartons for five years; plastic bags ten to 20 years; aluminium cans 50 to 100 years. Glass bottles sit there for a million years. And e-waste? In Australia, we chuck 578 000 tonnes a year. Imagine each tonne is equivalent to a small car. Then picture 600 000 of them parked in a field all together. Waste. Come back a year later and it's doubled. All your computer junk (some of it rejected only because it is last year's model, like a suddenly unfashionable frock) piled high. Sometimes it's sent to China. On a big ship. But now, no more.

In 2018, my friend Professor Veena Sahajwalla launched the world's first electronic waste microfactory. It extracts precious minerals from the waste and even has a 3D printing facility. She is the hero, by the way, who has managed to recycle the carbon of two million old tyres, in Australia alone, to make steel.

As for air travel, I put it under life's essentials, like having one or two babies. The Chinese (again!) tried a one-child policy and it didn't work, causing untold misery. And air travel, in terms of greenhouse gases, is now better than the carbon-cost of the internet and getting better all the time. Solar planes are flying and soon even the CEO of Qantas will agree, as has Richard Branson, that his company should include very fast trains and take up the challenge of routes such as Melbourne to Sydney (the fourth highest air traffic volume of any in the world) so as to cut the number of planes needed to fly.

Water is also a concern of mine. My behaviour is accordingly extreme and guaranteed to annoy. I keep a large saucepan in the kitchen sink to catch all hand washings, salad rinses and random drips and take the result several times a day to the garden or to flowers in vases and our many bird baths. This reminds me to look after thirsty plants and to go spare on water taps. Our water usage is heroically low. Not so our bills though, interestingly enough. As I write it's the driest September in New South Wales on record. Why waste a drop? Why pay more?

But, in case you want to emulate my saintly practice, be warned: do it when no one is looking or they will start muttering and looking up syndromes in psychiatric lexicons.

There is, however, a serious link between parsimony and effective environmental action. If you are too poor, as the folk in parts of Mexico and Indonesia obviously are, then the viciousness of squalor and the outrageous cost of thoughtless pollution are crippling. I have seen waterways in Mexico and (on film) in Indonesia so clogged with plastic and rubbish that the water itself is toxic and unusable. In Indonesia the incessant burning of peatlands and forests cleared to plant palm oil not only murders hundreds of thousands of people through foul air every year, it also kills the reefs. Smoke from fires descends on corals and chokes them and, in the process, destroys fisheries.

What's more it harms sea grasses. Is this a detail too far? No, sea grasses absorb and store 40 to 100 times more carbon dioxide than do tropical rainforests. This is *blue carbon* — it is a godsend and I say this as an atheist. Instead of dredging our coastline as we develop concrete shores where mangroves once stood, we could be restoring our natural riches and creating a calmer climate. Sea grasses also eliminate 50 per cent of the germs and plagues in coastal waters. Three magnificent benefits. Once more one can show that thinking green can save lives, money and industry (the fishing industry and tourism) whereas neglect costs so many lives all over our region.

Jane Lubchenco, President Obama's head of NOAA, mentioned earlier, who had spoken so incisively at the rally in Boston, told me in 2017 that they have studied the effect of preserving coastlines, sea grasses, mangroves and therefore fisheries, and discussed enterprises based on them with locals working in tourism, the sea and conservation. When they compared the wealth creation of that approach with one based on development (concreting the coastline), they found that the green approach yielded 30 per cent more income.

Slum children know the cost of everything and the value of much more. Their habits may be annoying but there is much more to consider. There is aesthetics: the elegance of tidiness. There is wealth: the richness of effective harmony. And there is progress: giving people room to move as the gridlock of squalor is broken.

War is the greatest creator of waste. George W Bush, reacting to 9/11, invaded Afghanistan and stayed. The cost is now US$3 trillion. Add Iraq.

Another old story. When we were in Vienna, living in the top flat of a typical European block of apartments, my little brother Shwn was just months old. During play, he dropped his teddy bear under the bed. For some reason (I was just over seven years old) I magnanimously went to fetch it. I looked underneath the bed. There was a pair of eyes looking back. There was someone *living* under the bed.

This was postwar Austria: the occupying troops were still marching through the broken streets and the pocks of gunfire still looked fresh on the walls of nearly every building. Shops sold little and the black market was pitiless. Though we were well off, I had already absorbed the desperation of the streets.

I retrieved the teddy and said nothing. I was being cool.

I asked Trudi, one of our nannies, in German — 'who is down there?' She was shaking as she told me: 'It is my sister. She's been there for three weeks. She has lived by giving blood but now she has run out of blood to sell and has nowhere to go.'

I told my parents, little shit that I was. However much I felt that woman's need, I preferred the attention given to a sneak. The sister went down to the cellar in the building's basement to live with the coal and the rats.

Even at age seven I knew what it was to be bereft. Slum child.

Oxford

I have many annoying habits, as I keep mentioning, annoyingly. One is to mention Oxford, gratuitously, when in certain company. The company includes friends and colleagues and consists of those with some fairly strong connections to that divine city.

Jonica was born there. Her father, David Newby, was a Rhodes Scholar. In fact Jonica, in her first moments alive at the Radcliffe Infirmary, managed to lose her father his scholarship — Rhodes sternly stipulated that his scholars be single and certainly not fecund. Meanwhile, Jonica's mother, after divorcing David, managed to marry yet another Rhodes Scholar, Lester, thus setting up some sort of record. Lester's college, Trinity, is opposite David's, Wadham, and right next to mine, Balliol. In fact, there is a puerile tradition at Balliol of slinging silly objects over the wall. Once, when resident at Balliol, I went next door to Trinity and said I was just going to inspect their long lawn to see whether it would suit as a Balliol car park. 'Yes, sir,' said the chap in the porter's lodge with a very straight face, 'we haven't heard that one for a couple of days now!'

My oldest friend with whom I attended grammar school, Michael Goldacre, got to Magdalen College in

1964, and is still there, as Professor Emeritus of Public Health. We married sisters. I was in Oxford twice with fellowships, and am still a member at Balliol. The founder of the ABC Science Unit, Dr Peter Pockley, was at Balliol for his doctorate. The new editor of science at the ABC, Jonathan Webb, technically my boss, was a Rhodes Scholar at Worcester College.

But one of the greatest attractions of Oxford for me is the complete absence of turmoil. All I've ever felt in Oxford is delight at the beautiful surroundings and a thrill for the intellectual buzz.

Every year I land at Heathrow, turn my back on London (who could stand going straight off the plane into the rush and the uproar of that too-large city?) and catch the coach to the Dreaming Spires. Just over 45 minutes later I'm wheeling my case into Balliol's front quad and the glorious silence of the ancient buildings and their sumptuous floral beds. Tall trees are beginning to lose their autumn leaves and squirrels lope across the grass. Old dons and young students smile as they stroll past, offering a welcome back.

It is a place to think, to recover, and relish.

The colleges themselves still enjoy their cherished eccentricities. Fellows get free meals every day during term time. This, I imagine, is based on the assumption that they are all, to the last, celibate resident monks with no family home to go to every evening. When the college is closed for a few weeks in the summer we are told which other college has been arranged to feed us in the interim. Imagine how many would otherwise starve. Dons have never been to the nearby Covered Market, a supermarket or a deli, let alone learned to cook, so they must walk an extra 200 yards to a hall with different portraits hanging to be served in the customary way. *Benedictus benedicat ...*

At Magdalen, when you go to dinner at High Table you first take sherry in the Senior Common Room, then you parade *along the roof*, entering the Hall through a window, then descend to the Table as others stand. After two courses you then repair to a special room where puddings, dessert wine and snuff are offered, the wine on a trolley pulled in one direction around the table on a rope. When I was there last, two women, new fellows, got fed up waiting for the trolley to be hauled in their direction (senior fellows were in intense conversation about the meaning of life at the end of the table and had not handed the rope onwards) and one woman got up and collected a bottle by hand. Shocked silence followed. 'Do you realise,' remarked our gowned host softly, 'that that's the first time this has happened in 400 years?' The trolley ritual had been shattered — but the Earth, surprisingly, still turned.

After pudding and snuff we all return to the Senior Common Room where I, as a guest, was weighed. 'You may like to know,' said Professor Sir Colin Blakemore, 'that you've put on nearly two stone since you last had dinner here ten years ago!'

Why, I once asked, do they weigh guests? We always have, came the answer.

Meanwhile, at my own college, Balliol, they claim, firmly, to be the oldest, not just in Oxford, but in Britain. On its 750th anniversary (the college was established in 1263) I went there to interview the deputy master, the chemist Professor John Jones. After going through some of the history I asked, 'Given the college is well over 750 years old, it occurs to me that *Doctor Who*, plainly of some kind of English stock given his accent, must have been to university around 700 years ago. Cambridge is too young. Obviously, he would not have attended either Paris or Bologna. Could he have been here at Balliol?'

'Undoubtedly,' Professor Jones replied without hesitation. 'After all, Captain Hook was here, wasn't he, after Eton, before he met Peter Pan. So why not *Doctor Who*?'

Only in Oxford.

*

My parents were keen for me to go to Cambridge. Accordingly, they gave me a list of their friends, correct-line dons, whom I should visit and impress. It was the last thing I wanted to do at 15 or 16. Their nagging continued, but then Gwyn died. Money was near non-existent in my family, so I drifted on, concentrating on banning bombs, enjoying jazz and skiffle and the company of girls.

Then Ray demanded I apply to Oxford. I explained I was not qualified — they then required Latin or Greek or, at least, an academically certified modern language, and I had none of these. But I applied anyway.

We did exam papers in the hall of Christ Church, surrounded by great pictures of great men. I blundered through. I was given an interview, of which I remember nothing. It was about that time that I learned that my headmaster had written to the college I'd applied for, Queen's (famous for Mr Bean and Tony Abbott), and said that under no circumstances was I to be considered a candidate — and that was that.

I doubt that I was then in any shape to handle Oxford. I left my temporary rooms opposite Iffley Road Track where Roger Bannister had broken four minutes for the mile and decided I would leave England after school. That, with poverty and the death of my father, was the greatest turmoil I endured growing up. Had I got into Oxford about twenty young people — my immediate and extended family — would not exist and life as a broadcaster wouldn't have happened. Gulp!

Michael Goldacre, who'd been as wayward as me, staying out all night, having adventures with girls and being chased by police for putting anti-government graffiti on Conservative Party walls, got a place at Magdalen College to read medicine. His former girl-friend Petronella Pulsford also got a place (she was formidably clever and incredibly glamorous). Shortly after going 'up' she joined the drama society OUDS and was promptly cast in *The Taming of the Shrew* alongside Richard Burton and Elizabeth Taylor.

The last time I saw 'Nelly', whose stage name was changed to Petronella Ford, she was playing Mrs Francis Crick in the BBC film of *The Double Helix*.

Michael became president of the Labour Club and played cricket for his college. In his medical training one figure stood out: Dr Hugh Sinclair. He appeared to be the classic don, combining apparent omniscience with unshakeable poise. He too loved cricket.

But appearances, to the young especially, deceive. As I was to find out much, much later.

*

On arriving off the plane from Sydney in the mid-1980s I received an urgent message from Michael Goldacre: 'You are needed to play cricket today at the Magdalen College ground in the annual doctors versus lawyers match. Turn up at midday — doesn't matter what you're wearing.'

I replied: 'But I've just spent 24 hours on a plane in economy and I haven't played any kind of cricket for a year, and *that* was with ten year olds!' But no excuses were accepted.

I showered, put on running gear and jogged to the grounds just beyond the University Parks. Now Magdalen has a long history and a deer park of renown as well as a magnificent chapel in which a version of Leonardo da Vinci's *Last Supper* used to hang. It is in much better condition than the original and at the right height to be appreciated fully as you look up. Magdalen also boasts an impressive list of alumni with, from Australia, Jack Eccles (of Nobel fame), Howard Florey (ditto), Malcolm Fraser, Gareth Evans (now chancellor of ANU), Ticky Fullerton (former presenter of ABC TV's business program) and from elsewhere: Oscar Wilde, CS Lewis, Andrew Lloyd Webber, Dudley Moore and Colin Blakemore.

It is also the college attended by Rebecca Richards, the first-ever Indigenous Australian Rhodes Scholar. She came from South Australia and was inspired to study anthropology and archaeology by stories her dad told her. She is now back doing research at the Natural History Museum in Adelaide. She had no bother with Oxford swank: she told me she was welcomed with warmth and enthusiasm 'because they didn't think we had a class system in Australia!'

As I arrived at the ground on that sunny, serene Sunday I saw Hugh Sinclair for the first time. He was unmistakable: dressed like a tramp (and, as a tramp myself, I notice this), he was surprisingly robust, despite his age. And it was remarkable how much he was being deferred to by the cricketers, who, as I was to find out, were a mixture of Law Lords, QCs, consultant physicians and surgeons from all over the nation.

I recall nothing of the match itself. I was not embarrassed exactly and may have scored two or three and not missed a catch, but as you'd expect, while fielding for the first time in years, I was surprised by the speed of the ball coming towards me over the grass and had to kick it to stop it rather than trust the quickness of my hands. I seem to remember that physiologist John Stein, brother of TV food star Rick, did rather well.

Everyone was pleasant and I was introduced properly to the long-time convener of the match, Dr Sinclair. He was extremely kind, noting my recent arrival that morning from the other side of the world, and said, apropos of my being a science journalist, that it was a pity I had not been there the day before as he'd hosted a board meeting of his Institute for Nutritional Research at his estate outside Oxford. Some of the notables playing that day had attended.

Dr Hugh Sinclair was a tutor in physiology at Oxford. You may never have heard of him but you do know his work. He was struck, in the 1940s, by the observation that Eskimos, as they were then called, thrived on a virtually all meat diet and, unlike western folk, showed no sign of the heart disease our own flesh is heir to. For various reasons he inferred that there was something in the fish and seal diet that was different from our own consumption of cow and sheep. He set out to investigate.

He bought a whole seal and lots of fish, took them to his lab and set out to eat nothing but for several weeks. He tested his blood at the same time. The smell from both the laboratory and his own body soon became too much for his colleagues and other Magdalen Fellows to bear and he was asked to desist. Eventually, he did, but not before finding something crucial that had eluded science until that point: the difference between saturated fats and unsaturated ones. The first are found in abundance in cattle and lambs, the latter in fish. This has influenced dieticians ever since. Sinclair became famous, as did his casual decision not to bother to write up his findings in a paper. Michael Goldacre and John Stein, among others, did this much later. But if you are at all aware of the health effects of eating fats, cholesterol and hardening of the arteries, think of Sinclair.

After the match, I suggested an interview for ABC Radio and Dr Sinclair was most enthusiastic. He invited me to his estate, Lady Place, the next day.

Lady Place was only a few miles' drive from Oxford and I found the gates to the grounds quite easily, two lions sitting regally atop tall pillars leading to spectacularly overgrown shrubbery beyond the entrance. Imagine Miss Havisham's house in *Great Expectations*, with equally bleak grounds. A few statues, eerily still, stood covered in mildew. Scruffy, wispy lawns held a marquee, silver tureens that had recently held piles of strawberries, and dozens of empty champagne bottles were strewn everywhere. There was a vast stone swimming pool with water so green you could see bubbles of gas erupting as if from a fetid pond deep in the woods. At the head of the pool lay Dr Sinclair, stark naked, his torso clearly trained with regular weights. The Tramp as Tarzan. He hurriedly sat up and found a towel to cover his loins.

We continued our affable conversation from the day before as if all was quite normal and he invited me to tour his 'Institute'. First, we entered the mock Tudor mansion. On the way in was a full suit of armour covered in cobwebs. Next came a large room in which stood a billiard table. On it was a model of the planned 'nutrition institute' — cardboard buildings and paper trees. Next to it, in pride of place, was a framed photograph of Dr Sinclair with a smiling Queen Mother.

Dust was everywhere. I made appreciative noises and we returned to a stone bench by the pool. We recorded an interview about non-saturated fats, diet and his plans, as well as the names of some of the lords (but no ladies) and professors who made up his institute's board.

Then I drove back to Oxford. There I sought out Colin Blakemore, at the time professor of physiology and an old friend with whom I could always talk frankly.

I came straight to the point. 'Colin, does Hugh Sinclair's institute actually exist?'

'No,' he replied. 'It is a whimsy of Hugh's and we all play along with it.'

'Then, you are telling me, Colin, that the great and the good from all over the nation come together every year and *pretend* they are dealing with a serious proposal when they know it's all baloney, then enjoy the champagne and strawberries?'

'Yes,' said Colin, 'this is Oxford, and everyone's very fond of Hugh.'

Charades in ancient places can be maintained for decades. Some think this is charming. Others believe it's bonkers.

When Dr Sinclair died in 1990 he left nothing to his old college. All his considerable wealth went to his Nutrition Institute. The head of Magdalen College at the time, ex-BBC man Anthony Smith, told me he was very cross about this snub. 'Sinclair didn't even leave us an old book!' Eventually the Hugh Sinclair Unit of Nutrition was set up, in 1995, in nearby Reading University (!) and the professor in charge, I note, is a Dr Christine Williams.

*

There is a problem with some British humour, particularly among men. It is used as a carapace, a means to pretend to be convivial, but without having properly to engage. I have known some Oxbridge types for many decades and never managed to have a personal conversation with them, despite trying. You know the image: three Oxford dons enter a bar (the Kings Head, maybe) and one says, 'Have you heard the one about the little boy who sees two dogs at it in the park? The boy says, "What are they doing, Daddy?"

'"Well," his father explains, "they are trying to make more puppies. That's how it's done."

'The next morning the boy blunders into his parents' bedroom while they too are playing hide the sausage. "What are you doing, Daddy?"

'Father goes puce and says, "Trying to make you a brother or a sister!"

'"Well," says the little boy, "can you turn Mummy over and try to make some puppies?"'

The three dons laugh with suitable gusto and turn to complaining about admin or the new dean, but never a word about real life. Such was Oxford in the twentieth century. It is different nowadays, largely. This could be because women are well established in all the colleges and the domination of high-functioning Asperger types and guffawing chaps from ancient family castles has been dissipated.

I have always enjoyed the humour, the ritualised jokes, but above all, the immediacy. You can end up very quickly at the heart of an issue. One day in 1993 I was discussing Chinese politics with a couple of my fellow Reuters journalists at Green College and was asking some abstruse question about how their university system was changing to accommodate the successes of western discoveries. I was told, 'Go around to St Anthony's College and you'll find two people who returned from

China yesterday who have been closely involved in that very problem.' I did. It worked. The same with most topics: there is always someone, around the corner, a world expert, delighted to see you if you are genuinely involved. As a world of ideas it is always exciting.

On my latest visit, in 2017, as I climbed into the (delayed) plane in Sydney setting out for the thirtieth or fortieth time to cross the world, I began to wonder whether this was sensible behaviour at my age. Across the world yet again! We landed at Heathrow about an hour late and I sped to the Oxford coach. A couple of hours later I was walking with my recorder to South Parks Road and the new, shining chemistry building. I asked for Vanessa Restrepo-Schild. She came to see me, smiling, a doctoral student from Colombia now resident at Christ Church (one is not supposed to call it a 'college'!) and we went to a room to talk. She had developed the ingredients for making an artificial retina. The first in the world! One day, when the medics have used her chemical marvel in animals and people and shown it works, she hopes it will enable those with macular degeneration and other blinding syndromes to see again. She was jolly, modest, South American, and represents the unexpected brilliance you keep finding in dear old, bright new Oxford. No wonder the *Times Education Supplement* has voted it once more the best in the world. Expect the unexpected.

One day in 1994, when I was based at Green College on my first fellowship venture to Oxford, someone I saw in the street asked, 'Are you coming to hear the talk by the Professor of Drama at St Cats [St Catherine's College]?'

'Err…Should I?' I asked, wondering which part of Oxford's obscurantist random referencing I was encountering.

'Well, it's Arthur Miller,' came the reply.

Right, off we go then. (Green College, by the way, is not named after environmental hardliners. It was funded, in part, by head of Texas Instruments, Cecil Green, and is entirely post-graduate. It is immediately next to the old Radcliffe Infirmary, where Jonica was born.)

Everything is within a three-minute walk in Oxford, so, having had nary a thought about drama when I got up that day, I was suddenly sitting opposite America's legendary playwright, former husband of Marilyn Monroe, in St Catherine's College, hearing about modern theatre and the influence of Shakespeare. Miller wrote one of America's most famous plays, *Death of a Salesman*, as well as its most contentious, *The Crucible*, on the persecution of the awkwardly different (leftists, perhaps?). I asked a question at the end, can't remember what about, but it was plausible and Miller gave me a fine answer. Afterwards a woman with an Australian accent approached me and said: 'You're Robyn Williams, aren't you, I recognised your voice.'

She turned out to be a lawyer from Canberra, at the time a leading fellow of Balliol College. Dr Jane Stapleton was her name and when in Australia she's a regular listener to ABC Radio and *The Science Show*. I explained I was on a Reuters Fellowship writing a book, and so she asked: 'Why not come to Balliol as a visiting fellow?' I replied that it is a rare privilege to be admitted to Oxford's oldest college and a place with a formidable intellectual tradition, I had as much chance as Donald Trump becoming president, but I could try.

She said she would look into it. Two years later, I was invited and said yes. All from a chance chat in the street about a drama lecture. Jane Stapleton, by the way, having since been a professor of law at the ANU, in 2016 became the first woman in history to become head of Charles Darwin's old college, Christ's in Cambridge. Incidentally, she has three doctorates, the first, from Adelaide, in chemistry.

And don't assume that traditional places such as Oxford and Cambridge are largely static. Not only is Professor Stapleton in the Master's Lodge at Christ's — go to the oldest college in Cambridge, Peterhouse, and there's another delicious surprise. That old pile, where much of Margaret Thatcher's High Tory cabinet were nurtured, also has a new 'Master'. She is BBC reporter and Russian scholar Bridget Kendall who, in 2016, moved into her college lodge with her partner, Amanda. There was no fuss.

The possibilities at great universities are almost limitless. You just have to get on with it. Perhaps I have a limited imagination, but I do not get put off by inhibitions about the grand. I have a variation of Groucho Marx's attitude ('I don't want to be a member of any club that will accept me as a member') in that I assume, if I am there, it can't be that special. The same applies to broadcasting. If I am in that studio on that day, superstar interview or not, million plus audience or not, then it can't be such a big deal with just me involved, so I just do it. Only in retrospect does the size of the crowd, the scale of the event, the fame of the guest seem overwhelming. How did I cope on the day? I downplay it: I am in a small room with a human being.

Pompous prigs and Hooray Henrys are obvious and you avoid them. This is what I tell newcomers to Oxford who may be a bit chary. There are always others who are worth meeting and talking to and in a large institution, plenty of them. Like the annoying parts of England as a whole, you leave the annoying ones be and look elsewhere. It's a big place, with lots to offer.

Oxford now has its first female vice-chancellor, Professor Louise Richardson. She has a PhD in terrorism. Both of us know how to handle a sometimes tricky iconic institution: we know where the villains are waiting.

This most ancient of universities has modernised and eccentrics (and cussed individualists) have become rarities. But turmoil besets even those hallowed halls. Brexit. Funds are crumbling. Many are giving up and leaving. The latest is my friend Sir Colin Blakemore, former head of the Medical Research Council and professor of physiology. He is moving to Hong Kong and saying goodbye, finally, to Oxford where he has done so much. It is sad indeed to watch this unnecessary upheaval.

Absent friends

Sir Talbot Duckmanton was a patrician from the old school. He smoked a pipe, went to his club, Tattersalls, at lunchtime, and maintained the polite but firm standards of the Australian grandee. For 18 years he was general manager, a role now briskly called CEO, of the ABC. He was the first of my nine supreme bosses. So far.

Eighteen years is a very long time for a top executive. Today you get about five, perhaps eight. But the ABC, when I joined in 1972, was a commission, part of the public service. The federal minister was the Post Master General and many of the technicians we worked with were still, kind of, post office engineers, and *they* were allowed to touch equipment such as editing machines and we weren't.

Nonetheless, out of sight in the Science Unit, we had our own gear and cut tape and produced programs on the sly, and management pretended not to see. It was another age. Duckmanton had come up through News and Sport and, it was said, had been one of those, before instant satellite transmission, who'd faked Test cricket broadcasts from abroad by reading from printed messages sent by telegraph and accompanying them with noises made by hitting a pencil on a table, as if a shot had sent the ball to the boundary. Duckers, as we called him between ourselves, arrived at Broadcast House in Elizabeth Street every morning (the ABC in Sydney was a vast diaspora of buildings with TV on the North Shore and radio and management all over the city) to be greeted by a staff commissionaire. He would say 'Good morning, Mr Duckmanton,' and tip his lid. One day, myth has it, the general manager after a decade or so of this ritual said, 'Oh, come on, Harry, you don't have to be quite so formal.' So, Harry straightaway said, 'Oh well, then good morning, Mr Duck.'

In later years, as the lively sixties and stroppy seventies brought rapid industrial change and the ABC became a corporation, we went through strikes and upheavals and Duckmanton left. We moved to a new HQ in Ultimo.

That was 1991. Having been ensconced in our various offices, but not yet joined by TV, I had a thought. Had Tal (we no longer called him Duckers — too Pommy) seen the new premises? I was already an old-timer, having been in the broadcasting organisation for nearly 20 years and I knew most of our main people. Though I and my mates had been disruptive and even industrial in our careers, we liked to keep a sense of decorum and friendliness while we were at it. So, it was that at the end of one of our strikes, in 1978 I think it was, when the airwaves had gone silent, I nonetheless invited the entire ABC board, the 'enemy', to the Science Unit Christmas party, which was a famous annual event in those days, attended by hundreds of colleagues. The *entire* board came, led by John Norgard and Dame

Leonie Kramer. There was not a shadow of disdain — yes, we had fought but we were nonetheless *family*. I even proposed a toast to Marius Webb, our staff-elected commissioner (this position had been one of the points of contention in the strike) and the board raised their glasses and drank with a smile to the Christmas spirit. There was still goodwill in the 1970s and 1980s. What would the 1990s bring? I was about to find out. (Now in 2018 I would be unlikely to recognise more than one or two members of the ABC board — from their pictures in the newspaper!)

So, what had happened to Tal? I consulted Marius, the hairy pixie who, in 1974, had been one of the three who had invented the youth network 2JJ, soon to be Triple Jay, and run the rock station with élan before returning to Radio National. Then I found ace broad-caster Tim Bowden, first executive producer of *PM*, who had pioneered social history broadcasting with legendary series on Changi and Antarctica, *and*, signifi-cantly, had proposed, with me, no-confidence motions against Duckmanton and the board during the strikes. Next Paul Murphy, who hosted *PM*, and finally I found Roger Grant, another frontline reporter who'd been an international correspondent and headed our US bureau.

Always consult the folk who are likely to disagree with you. Shall we ask Tal for tea and a tour? They hummed and hah-ed, but then agreed; he may have been an old pipe-smoking git, but he was our git. So, I wrote him a letter, naming my friends and saying come for an informal cuppa and a chat, or a royal tour, whatever suits. We shall arrange.

The reply was not swift but came soon enough, carefully typed on occasionally whited-out notepaper. I present it here in, for me, all its shocking detail. I had thought Tal would be comfortable in retirement, like General de Gaulle, ready to emerge, as stature and contemporary events demanded, to his natural place on the national stage. Not so. He had been consigned to the ash can of history.

Dear Robyn

Thank you very much for your courteous and friendly letter of 30th October.

You will, I'm sure, understand that so much has happened in the field of broadcasting and in the ABC in the last nine or ten years, that it is a little difficult for me to respond to your letter except in a purely social sense. I appreciate your suggesting that I might meet you with Roger and Marius; but I think a profitable exchange of views at any level on current broadcasting matters, or indeed in the area of past history, might well leave us all a little perplexed, even though we have an extensive vocabulary of shared references.

What I must make quite clear is that I have no wish whatsoever to 'pay a visit to the ABC' either formally or informally. It is too late for that and the reason is quite simple. In the years that have passed since I chose to retire, and during which time I have declined all requests to comment publicly on broadcasting matters, no senior ABC executive or board member has sought to make contact with me, nor have I been invited to any ABC function with the exception of a concert to mark the inauguration of the Charles Moses Foundation and more recently the opening of the Ultimo complex. I have not even received a copy of the Corporation's annual report! In fact the only correspondence I have had from an ABC source since 1983, apart from your letter, has been brief notes to cover despatch copies of obituary notices published in the British press when former BBC and ITV friends have died and which, in the absence of other contacts, give me cause to think that, apart from anything else, I am being subtly reminded of the brevity of life. There is only one conclusion to be drawn from all this … and I have drawn it. What I remember referring to somewhat facetiously as 'the obscurity of retirement' several years ago, has been redefined for me.

So while I do very much appreciate the kindliness and the convivial spirit which prompted your letter, and without wishing to appear in any way discourteous, may I simply thank you and your colleagues for thinking of me and the suggestions you have made. Perhaps, at a later date we can pursue further the possibility of a quiet, private 'rendez-vous'.

Yours sincerely,
Tal D

He died four years later. We never did meet again.

Why does this matter? It shows to me an organisation, like many in Australia today, increasingly willing to ignore its own history, its human past. This is reinforced nearly every week at the ABC by other 'retirements' and the disappearance of those who've been so familiar for years.

Is the concept of a career out of date? How do you plan, as a young person, for a world where you are told half the jobs of the future haven't been invented yet? How dare they tell our kids things like that? The present turmoil is bad enough without having the floor fall away.

What I tell them is to choose an education offering the greatest range and flexibility: science (STEM) looms large in this advice, despite the thoughts of the New South Wales Minister for Education. My argument is that nature surrounds us perforce and so any job must involve knowledge of it. But you must also build up *experience*. How do you do that when job security is so ephemeral?

Duckmanton and I are, oddly enough, examples of the way skills accumulate. He came up through the ranks and, like so many great journos, was steeled by the turmoil of war reporting. I was running around drama and light entertainment studios for years while studying and had already spent a decade or more exploring the world the rough way. We had both 'left the building'. We knew the world.

But what about Flaubert's dictum that to be 'violent and original in your work' required the basis of an orderly life? Being jostled through endless uncertainties of earning a buck is no way to be creative or even productive. No wonder all those workers here and in the USA voted with their two fingers in the air. Without secure work you are nowhere. Confidence evaporates, friends lose touch, and those once vital skills start to fade. The only plus is that you are finally spared the worry of being 'let go' and having to read all those corporate emails and slogans about how important you are as a person to the corporation.

Is it the same, sitting at home, blogging away, convincing yourself that independence is the new belonging and that going to work is in the ash can of history? It seems to me that this is a fraud.

History matters; corporate memory is priceless. The best way to invent the future is to build on the best of the past. It's how civilisations flourish.

E-life doesn't help. You can deceive yourself that you are in touch because you are e-connected. If that is working and our next generation of Australians is better informed than ever, then why are our figures plunging by comparison with international standards? Especially in STEM subjects. Why did the chairman of Dow Chemicals, Australian-born Andrew Liveris, who briefly chaired President Trump's Manufacturers Committee, warn that this country risks becoming a nation of 'hamburger flippers' if we don't look to our educational standards? He listed the countries rapidly moving ahead and reminded us of those concerns Barry Jones had in the 1980s in his book *Sleepers, Wake!* on looking forward to a technological revolution and its new jobs. It seems we've still not woken up.

Our students are choosing commerce, law, media,

economics — the very fields open to greatest uncertainty as markets fragment and collapse. And so many of them seem to know … very little.

'Have you heard of HG Wells?' I ask, the man who helped invent science fiction, created STEM, wrote *War of the Worlds* (the film of which starred Tom Cruise), the story of which was inspired by the European invasion of Tasmania, and who was instrumental in warning Churchill about possibilities of an atomic bomb. No? What about Florey? Edith Cowan? No, despite her being on your money. OK, so let's just do some more clickbait: what are the ten favourite iDevices for 20 year olds in Oz in 2017? We are, after all, keen to score the young audience.

I do want younger folk to listen. So, I put them on. And they don't look at me blankly saying 'What is a radio?' or 'What is a script?' Quite the opposite. Most are immensely pleased to find themselves on national radio, which is also international radio. They get a huge response, not least from overseas, and tell me how grateful they are. And I ask them to tweet everyone they've ever met and tell them to listen or podcast the show. Hence the rather lovely ratings.

One encounter stands out. I was at the launch of a book, a graphic novel called *The Secret War* all about a germ, dysentery, in the tummy of a nurse in World War I. It told how disease caused more deaths than bullets in that appalling conflagration a hundred years ago. The person launching the book was Ted Baillieu, former premier of Victoria. Among the audience was a 15-year-old schoolgirl. I asked her what she was doing there and she said she was very interested in science. Her name was Zofia.

After the speeches I asked her whether she fancied writing something for my program *The Science Show*. She immediately said yes. I returned to Sydney.

Less than a week later, my computer went *ping* and Zofia's name came up. She had indeed written a short talk, plus a poem, all about Cecilia Payne. The latter, some will know, was the first woman to get a tenured chair in physics at Harvard. Payne had elucidated the role of hydrogen in the cosmos as the basis for the formation of stars.

How did Zofia know all this? It turned out that she listened to ABC Radio programs (especially those about science) when doing woodwork with her mother! And what did her mother do? She used to be in Circus Oz. Every week I am finding extraordinary young people, brimming with talent and enthusiasm, desperate to be offered leadership and direction in this famously changing world. I broadcast them all the time. They are an inspiration. It is their talents that should be recognised and directed, not regarded as nerdy or faintly eccentric. They are the ones to lead us from present turmoil. Liveris is right — we risk becoming a nation of numbskulls rather like the one I encountered back in 1964, the land of Bazza McKenzie.

*

Let me give two more examples of the young people I have found pioneering good ideas in unlikely places.

The first is the Hacking Shed in Launceston. Go to that city in the middle of Tasmania and you will find a large museum set in the converted remains of a railway yard. Beyond the main building are many sheds and in two of them a bunch of entrepreneurs in the computer industry have set up some technology, old and new, which schoolkids can come and use. They have the old-fashioned bulky gear to take apart and fiddle with plus the cutting-edge stuff of the mini-black-box variety, including the latest versions of virtual reality in which you can place yourself at the feet of moving dinosaurs or within Van Gogh's own kitchen next to his famous chair.

The kids experiment with real projects: electronic guides to show you where to find exhibits within the museum, or simulators enabling you to control and drive locomotives, watching a screen as if you're at the controls in the cabin. They are learning both how to run and code computers and, significantly, how to get on with bosses in business long before they have left school.

Still in Launceston, I met a team of undergraduates who had designed autonomous vehicles and were competing internationally at the highest level. This was *before* they'd actually finished their first degrees.

I found similar enterprise at the University of Sydney, where Harry Steel, also an undergraduate, was designing rockets together with their satellites and competing in America with the best. His friend Gaia Hermann, meanwhile, was putting together new DNA to make hitherto unknown forms of life: organisms that could be useful in all sorts of ways. Such young folk are as smart as you'd wish to find anywhere; all they need is a place to go when qualified: *somewhere*. That last bit is up to us.

*

But the contempt for history is rife and especially apparent among those who don't read books. One of the failings of recent governments in Australia, let alone the USA, has been the firing of experienced public servants whose collective memories are thus sent into a kind of oblivion. The political editor of the *Australian Financial Review*, Laura Tingle, now on ABC TV, has written compellingly about this fault. It produces a generation of those with a proud ignorance of all that came before and so comes with a catastrophic tendency to repeat old errors. No wonder international affairs are such a mess. You know the old line: 'War is God's way of teaching Americans geography.' Such a waste.

Which brings me back to Tal. In his letter Sir Talbot had a final paragraph and it said this:

> In the meantime, let me urge you to try again
> to persuade Earle Hackett, one of the best
> Commissioners we ever had incidentally, to resume
> writing and broadcasting regularly. My powers of
> persuasion have, so far, failed. To me, it's tragic that
> his considerable talents as a communicator are not
> being used.

Dr Earle Hackett, a world expert on blood, came from Adelaide, via Ireland, and was the Radio Doctor before

Norman Swan. He was indeed on the board of the ABC and, in fact, became chairman when the previous one died on 11 November 1975. (Few noticed because, as you may recall, that was, doubly, a momentous day in Australian history.) Earle wrote wonderful scripts, funny, often outrageous, and packed with brilliant scientific ideas. When Earle died I broadcast one of his delightful stories about the time he was a medical student doing rounds with other students. A gruff professor noticed Earle dreamily looking out of the window, seemingly oblivious to the patient in the bed.

'Hackett,' he boomed, 'what conclusions have you reached so far?' Earle was blank, stuttered, made something up, fell silent. 'Right, Hackett, we shall continue rounds with those who are awake. Meanwhile, examine this patient and see whether he has red marks on his knees.'

'Right, prof,' said Earle, becoming suddenly a student of action. The patient now had his full attention.

Ten minutes later the professor returned with his student retinue. 'Well, Hackett? Your diagnosis?'

'Well,' replied young Earle with assurance, 'it seems he hasn't read Marx on his knees — nor standing up either.'

We do miss Earle, some of us. And, in a different way, Sir Talbot as well. When Tal died his daughter told me, much to my amazement, that the letter I sent more than 25 years ago was one of the high points of his later years.

An organisation that forgets its history has lost its heart. Emailed messages from on high are not a substitute.

Loss

Is there a more profound turmoil than death? In my more than 40 years with the ABC I have lost too many important colleagues — Peter Luck (*Four Corners*), Peter Pockley (founder of the Science Unit), Halifax Szevcyk (my first producer), Peter Hunt (our brilliant environment reporter on *The Science Show*) and Alan Saunders (broadcaster and writer) to name a few.

Two of the heaviest losses occurred within a month of each other in 2017: John Clarke (April) and Mark Colvin (May). This, and the next chapter, is what I wrote the day each of them died.

*

Fred Dagg is dead. What a vile world. Some souls should be spared, even if the gods do love them.

The first thing to understand about John Clarke is that he was a genius. He cherished words and used them in such wonderful ways: as a big beery singer; as a sensitive poet; as a sheep shearer in wellies singing to the stock; as a screenwriter (Remember *The Games*? Wow!); as a slightly amused politician sitting with Bryan Dawe, never missing a beat, never recording a bummer; and as a conversationalist. On every subject you could pick.

My partner Jonica phoned him in Melbourne for the first time in 2016, a little nervously, and an hour later was still laughing happily, chatting away. They were procrastinating, they both confessed, delightedly. Something both did so well.

Such was the brilliance of *The Games*, a satire preceding the Sydney Olympics of 2000, that not only did we see the foibles of bureaucracy on display, a forerunner of Working Dog's *Utopia* series, but also the exquisite originality of lines that questioned, for example, why the 100 metres events had to be 100 metres. Some smart suit had changed it, of course, to fit another contingency. Times change! We must follow the mission statement, not some nerdy definition of a metre. Isn't it French, after all?

The second thing is that John's comedy and satire may have been as cutting as a laser beam, but it was never snide or bilious. He was there for the fun and the gentle send-up — far more effective than the steel-capped boot.

The third thing was his scholarship. Read his classical works rewritten. They capture the essence of every artist he emulated and, as spoken by him, even more so. He was a magnificent Dylan Thomas: '*There were uncles, always the uncles …*' he boomed in a take-off of 'A Child's Christmas in Wales'.

Fourth, John was an improviser. This was useful when yet another deadline whooshed past him. I once met him in the old ABC studios in Melbourne in the snug atrium of the rather cottagey building, and he was scribbling away with a biro. I saw he'd managed three lines of what was supposed to be a ten-minute soliloquy.

'How's it going?' I asked.

'Atrocious,' he replied.

So, we sloped into the studio and winged it. The topic was the meaning of life. He was beyond brilliant. My role was to contain my boiling laughter and to try not to snort and end up with an internal haemorrhage, it was so funny. I like to think it was a trial run for *Clarke and Dawe*.

Fifth, he was an athlete. I once invited him to a beach in Mount Eliza which turned out to be a nudist beach. He wore a bowler hat and nothing else and we threw Frisbees. His were as accurate as Exocet missiles heading straight for one's parts. And he was built like an All Black.

Sixth, John was also a science man. He worked with top scientists from the Australian Academy of Science on the wellbeing of Western Port Bay. He persuaded schoolkids to be involved and was delighted when teachers allowed them to play in the sloppy mud and sand, planting mangrove saplings. He saw the horror of the children when, the next day, they found some hoons had trashed the lot, dug them up and flung them. So, John and his mates did a report on ABC TV's *7.30*, showing the schoolkids that most of us cared, and they replanted the baby trees the next day. John took photos as they went — he was an inspired natural history photographer.

Seventh, John was a great friend, especially to women. Jonica idolised him. He and his wife, Helen, a distinguished fine arts scholar, were blissfully close.

And there are so many more qualities. He was

another example of that unique Aussie — the New Zealander. We claim him with pride, along with Russell Crowe, Jane Campion, Janet Frame, Sam Neill and Ernest Rutherford. He was a trouper who performed with the best of our comedy teams and led them to ever more hilarious outrages (remember Gillies?), always with that wonderfully straight face and tiny twinkle. And he cared about the ABC, even as he sent it up pitilessly. He was a hoaxer, and we sold the national broadcaster (in one of our *Science Shows*) to Kerry Packer, broadcast the fabulous farnarkling finals, discovered the fossilised beer can and worried about the ethics of sheep until management had breakdowns.

We have lost a real national treasure and so have the Kiwis.

But Fred Dagg is not dead. Nor John Clarke. He will delight us on the airwaves forever.

Public service broadcasting

My Mark Colvin story begins in 1974. I was in London, having decided to return there after an enjoyable two years mucking about in Sydney and the ABC. I had the fanciful idea that I'd offer myself to the BBC and they would wilt with joy at the opportunity to enlist me and thrust open all doors. Meanwhile I carried on as if still a Talks Officer Grade Zilch with Oz Auntie (they had no idea I was planning to leave) and proceeded to collect interviews — not only with scientific subjects but wherever the imagination and intellectual curiosity took me. I had already, having been with the ABC for only two years, recorded features on the Irish Famine, Michael Foot's biography of Aneurin Bevan, and on the origins of war. Yes, we had no silos back then. You did your speciality and whatever else came up and I am amused these days when I hear our managers' entreaties to break out of our boxes. In those days you did the lot. Many of us still do.

And on this day in London I was walking down Piccadilly to Albany, the exclusive apartment block, on my way to interview Lord Clark of *Civilisation* fame.

Kenneth Clark had become famous in 1969 as the presenter of this 13-episode series on big ideas dreamed up by David Attenborough in one of his masterstrokes on becoming, briefly, a TV executive. Today it is being redone as *Civilisations* with Mary Beard, David Olusoga and Simon Schama. I had enjoyed *Civilisation*. It had direct, plain language, a handy briefing for namedroppers (like me) on what is supreme in classical art and where it came from, and a guide whose scholarship was beyond question. Yes, he left out plenty of art from anywhere east or south of Constantinople — but, frankly, how many foreigners could the average chap really cope with in the 1960s?

I'd read Clark's memoirs with delight. Apart from all that reprehensible name-dropping he was criticised for, I was touched by one surprising confession: when the noble lord, however scholarly, set foot in a new exhibition or was about to see a great work by a leading artist, he was invariably moved to tears. The great man cried for that which he loved! I found this remarkable and it made me like him more than ever. I too am moved to tears by aspects of nature, fine music and great achievement.

And I liked certain other personal touches in his writing, like the way he revealed his secrets of how to talk to a camera. He had the habit of musing to himself about paintings, sometimes out loud, as he strolled through the woods and countryside. 'Done this for years,' he confessed. All he then had to do for telly was to time the reflections and look sincerely into the lens. I had adapted the Clark technique myself by walking around and around a tree. You talk aloud until the phrases stick, then look down the barrel and say it again. My only snag, as Jonica would point out when directing me, is that I concentrate on the words so intensely I frown and look as if I want to kill the viewer. The noble lord was much more engaging.

Kenneth Clark opened the door of apartment B5 in Albany and invited me in. He was not put off by my long hair and general appearance of a guitarist in a garage band. Next he did something that's confounded me ever since: he offered me a large glass of scotch.

'Bit early!' I mumbled.

'Well, you're a journalist,' he replied.

It was 10 a.m. We chatted. I was there to ask him about aspects of his memoirs (which I imagine is how I managed to get to see him in the first place). But before I could set up my large recorder, a knock took him back to the front door and I was left with my whisky to contemplate the room.

Albany is comfortable but not too spacious. Clark's drawing room was, of course, full of artworks, most of them small. I was staggered to find I was alone with numerous priceless portraits by Goya. How easy it would have been to slip one into my case. Clark was both generous and trusting.

The interview was fine — I recall little of what he said — but my generalities in questioning him about the march of human progress were met by aperçus of appropriate originality with not a cliché to mar the ever-so-elegant delivery.

And so back to Sydney. And immediately a request from one of our evening programs on ABC Radio, *Broadband*, to broadcast what I'd brought back. *Soon*. I wonder whether there would be the same eagerness in 2017 to put such highfalutin reflections to air.

But there was a problem. No producer. We in ABC Radio were, back then, in a diaspora of buildings around Kings Cross and William Street among the hookers, trannies and spag shops of the red-light district. The studios of Upper Forbes Street, just up from the Wall, where giant fellows in drag would wait after twilight, were shared by broadcasters from all ABC networks and I had secured somewhere to put my Clark feature together but could not do so alone.

Then I spotted a tall, slim young man hanging about doing not very much and I asked him to help. 'Just sit and listen, watch the levels and make sure I don't read too quickly,' I instructed and mumbled something about the topic, not expecting an overgrown teenager to know much about civilisation or Lord Clark.

'Yes,' said Mark Colvin, 'I saw him in Oxford. I've read his books.' I stared in disbelief. The voice was precise and clearly educated — but what was its owner doing in the ABC? And, it turned out, working in News for a rock station, 2JJ?

The recording done, we chatted. As is customary with Brits, I checked his pedigree and found he'd been at one of the great independent schools, Westminster, where sons of diplomats were wont to be sent. Mark's dad was one such. Then he'd gone to Oxford, Christ Church, following Lewis Carroll, WH Auden and any number of British prime ministers. No wonder he knew about Clark.

We became friends. I was surprised to find he'd chosen journalism with no particular training in the field, nor any experience. But, like me, he'd travelled widely and had adventures, good and bad, in faraway places, from trying to eat goat's ear in Mongolia — being polite to his father's hosts while trying not to throw up — to using several languages all over Europe as snipers fired. We both also read books, incessantly. There was no topic that stumped him.

His broadcasting was built on a command of words, usually simple ones carrying a punch. Don't write fornicate with three syllables, write fuck. Don't say Marxist-Leninist revolutionary, say commie. His specialisation, on leaving the nursery of 2JJ, became foreign affairs. He was posted to London, Belgium (where I stayed with him and his wife Michelle and young son Nick more than once) and reported from all over Asia and, ominously, Africa.

The other ABC reporters loved him. Why? Here was someone tall and imposing, with tones like a toff, who was nonetheless at one with the mateship of the Aussie journo style, male and female. The answer is straightforward: Mark Colvin had not one iota of bullshit in his then-elegant frame. He was dedicated to public service broadcasting. He enjoyed satire and fun. He loved what he did and it showed. He also loved to share the treasures of experience. After he died there was an outpouring of tributes from every broadcaster imaginable praising Mark's role as mentor and inspiration. There was Tony Jones, decades ago, at that time a minor hack on a lowly local paper, hearing one of Mark's evocative broadcasts from a war zone and deciding, on the spot, to try to follow his example and become a foreign correspondent, whatever the barriers. Tony came in to News and

Current Affairs at the ABC, did his broad apprentice-ship, then went to London and Washington from which he was posted to war zones such as Bosnia. When he spoke of that inspiring day listening to Mark's evocative report, Tony was moved to tears. The other quality his peers recognised was that Mark never gave up.

But what about that public service broadcasting? Isn't it as dated as the Raj? Well, it is to some. But not to most of us. You do things for the common good, one defined by the public itself. It is no fluke that the ABC is the most trusted organisation in Australia, as they keep reminding us. Many surveys have shown, almost without fail, that public service broadcasters' efforts are valued and shown to underpin democracy, education and the essentials of a vibrant culture. Only when our programs are debauched in imitation of commercial shows do we find listeners and viewers fade away. There are many elements of that public service in those famous programs made by Lord Clark and David Attenborough. We need to know about science, about art, Africa, Brexit, about the machinations of noisy foreigners, because one day an obscure (to us) land far away will be somewhere our children will be having to defend. Or feed. Or fear. And that's why Mark was prepared to pack his swag and fly off yet again to countries where corpses were piled as high as those mountains of discarded tyres, with flies and vermin running everywhere. Not for kicks. For you.

He caught a germ in Rwanda when reporting on the awful genocide. The auto-immune disease wrecked his body and it was Dr Norman Swan who was on the phone straightaway organising the right doctors to be on standby in London to receive Mark as he flew, broken, back to base. This saved his life. He lay for months in hospital, receiving colossal doses of cortisone, which would eventually ruin his hip joints and kidneys. But he survived, came back to Australia, and, inevitably, returned to work.

He'd already been there way back to launch *The World Today* on ABC Radio (I'd helped persuade him to host the show) and now he was set to present *PM*. That splendid voice, molasses with brandy, that authority, gravitas with grace, genuine curiosity, erudition with eagerness, became part of our Australian households over the next 15 years. He was often absent as the operations followed each other: new hips, failing kidneys, too much dialysis. But he always came back.

The sensations kept coming. His father died and turned out, in Mark's words, 'to be a spook'. He wrote a book about it, part memoir, part portrait of his dad, the man from MI6. *Light and Shadow* became a bestseller. Then came the play *Mark Colvin's Kidney* starring the actor John Howard as Mark. (Such an irony!) It told the story of phone-hacking and gutter journalism, how Elle Macpherson's PA had been framed as a leaker and how she, Mary-Ellen Field, had met Mark during his coverage of the scandal. They both had the same rare blood group: A-rhesus negative. She made the offer of a kidney. He refused. She persisted. His life was saved for the second time.

Mark was embarrassed by the play's title (it was *her* kidney), and annoyed by being portrayed as occasionally demanding. 'I never ask someone to fetch me a glass of water!'

By now the slim youngster had ballooned into a blimp as the cortisone and immune suppressors did their work. When he came to dinner with us in 2016 after he'd wrapped the second edition of that night's *PM*, he entered with a stick, lurching forward slowly, twice the size he should have been. But, once seated, he joined the conversation with courtesy and zest (a rare combination). Then he hit the wall and was off. One of the best pieces of advice he gave me when I became very ill (from cancer and chemo) was not to endure company beyond coping. When you feel weak, *go*. There is no point persevering when you are that sick. Explain, briefly, and retire early.

The drugs preventing him from rejecting his new kidney eventually did too much damage and Mark was told, in early 2017, that he had lung cancer. He was suddenly not on air, but the cause was kept under wraps. He died on 11 May 2017.

Ten minutes after I heard the news I was asked to go on the ABC TV News to pay tribute. It was not easy to do but I thought: 'Mark would just go on and do it.' When I got home mid-afternoon to prepare for an event that night, a farewell for John Cleary (we have plenty of farewells at the ABC), I saw an email requesting a few pars to put on a website about Mark. I wrote something quickly, told the story, briefly, of Lord Clark and meeting Mark for the first time. I ended, rather whimsically: 'Send us one last tweet Mark. You know you can.' During his attendance for dialysis for hours, two to three times a week, Mark had become a fervent tweeter, passing the time, recommending articles, giving news, offering advice. He had thousands of followers.

An hour after I wrote those words, would you believe, there came that last tweet. Mark had found a way to have his final message go out just an hour after he died. It said, 'It's all been bloody marvellous.'

Says it all.

Evil

One of the crucial ingredients of turmoil is terminal frustration. I feel it myself more than I'd like. What's the point? Time to give up? Time to rage, seeking revenge? Have we, finally, come to be ruled by fanatics who cannot be redeemed?

I think the actions of the Republicans opposing everything President Obama wanted to do, irrespective of merit, was evil. I think that the man who drove into pedestrians in central Melbourne in January 2017, killing five and injuring many more, is evil; the same for the truck driver who ploughed into a crowd in Nice the year before. Evil. So are the zealots who destroyed Palmyra.

I think Trump's wilful ignoring of climate science and the underpinnings of environmental regulation in America is evil, as is the policy on capital punishment in parts of the USA, Indonesia, China and Thailand.

The list could go on; so, I'm sure, could yours.

But philosophers tell us it is false to ascribe the word evil to such things as it implies they have an essential and immutable nature. So, saying Hitler was evil, or anyone else likewise, gives us nowhere to go. Without World War I, bad potty training, a testicle deficiency and the vengeful penalties the Allies imposed upon a defeated

Germany, Little Adolf could have turned out nothing more than an average twitchy housepainter with bad prose. Another man in the street of no consequence. Trump and the Republicans, it's feasible, could somehow be persuaded to be more flexible in the national interest; and those murderous young men who kill strangers for fun may, in fact, be mad and therefore treatable. Or misled and one day remediable. Evil, they say, is a dead end. No human is a dead end.

But there comes a level of bloody-mindedness that, surely, allows us at least to borrow evil as a metaphor. After all, the new PM of Britain once called her Tories 'the Nasty Party'. Nasty is quite close to evil. And there was something similar in the infamous utterance by Margaret Thatcher that 'there is no such thing as society'. That surely was beyond nasty.

Except both women actually said something rather more subtle. Theresa May said: 'There is a lot we need to do in this party of ours. Our base is too narrow and so, occasionally, are our sympathies. You know what some people call us: the Nasty Party.' She was addressing the Conservative Party conference in Bournemouth in 2002. It seems a reasonable, indeed an enlightened attitude: *others are saying we are beastly and we need to take notice.*

As for Thatcher, she too was being more equivocal. She actually said: 'I think we've been through a period where too many people have been given to understand that if they have a problem, it's the government's job to cope with it … They're casting their problem on society. And, you know, there is no such thing as society. There are individual men and women, and there are families. And no government can do anything except through people, and people must look to themselves first.'

Thatcher was challenging the culture of entitlement back in 1987. She was asking neighbours, friends and family to step in first, before we invoke the machinery of the state, which could be too remote, too slow and even insufficient. She may have been wrong, at least in part, but was she evil?

Perhaps, like me, you are amused by the contradictions so characteristic of the hard right. They require the rule of law but hate regulation; demand personal liberty but condemn the rainbow society with its gays and free love; want Christian charity to prevail but insist that the poor and oppressed pull themselves up by their own frayed, tattered, puny bootstraps. Or just go away. Especially if they are foreign. Good Samaritans be damned, this is the Real World. They are pro-life but execute crims at an industrial level.

That attitude can be annoying but it is not ultimately evil. Slavery was and is remediable. There are ways to deal with its awful origins and manifestations. If William Wilberforce and others had believed slaves were a necessary evil like so many British sugar planters and half of North America, abolition may never have been achieved.

But I still like to use the word, if only for dramatic impact. It focusses attention. It shocks. So I say again: the Tea Party is evil, so are men who beat women.

What is more interesting is to ask how this nasty ingredient comes to manifest itself in an otherwise civil society and what makes otherwise hedonistic, unremarkable young men turn into driven fanatics.

Consider a hypothetical case: a young man called Jet (let's not be too didactic and coin a name with religious baggage). Jet displays all the characteristics of an undirected, half-educated, barely matured kid — traits shared by millions. Males are more crassly juvenile for their age than females, less articulate, deceptively dense given their size and aggression. They are pretend adults and they are dangerous.

But Jet gets by through self-indulgence: the usual cocktail of illicit powders, cheap grog, street fights and occasional rape. Raves include nicking cars and doing burnouts. His 'living' is underpinned by petty crime and scrounging.

Ultimately, he is bored. The brain is unstimulated and Jet's street gang amounts to very little, unlike the bikie brotherhoods with their traditions, elaborate rules and motor pride. So he is drifting, and the boy-hedonism simply fills the grey days.

Along comes a radical indoctrinator offering a life purpose and a rigid set of rules. Jet is no longer to be a piece of young flotsam, he will be a *warrior*. His brain is still unformed (it won't be mature for ten years when he's 30, later than with women) and he is open to intense indoctrination as well as a tendency to obedience. His parents may find this surprising but they let their offspring go feral years ago. For the first 200000 years of human existence the tribal elders gave boys challenging rites of passage and there was no choice about bungee jumping off the high platform (Vanuatu) or grappling with the wild beast (South Africa). Survival for the next generation meant having a mind that bent to the will of your elders. On the streets of the West such leadership is absent during peacetime. There you find only influences likely to reinforce thuggery: bands of brothers forming tribes; bored youths seeking thrills just to feel alive; substances to mash the brain and abolish relationships beyond the gang.

What always puzzled me was the willingness of Jet and other young hedonists to turn so readily to asceticism: no more drugs, booze, even music in some cases. Is there something in our male brains that can switch to obedience? Is it a tendency to bow to the leader of the tribe (daddy?) that overrules everything else?

Damian Scarf, who lectures in psychology at the University of Otago in New Zealand, has experimented with two groups of young men: one comprising teenagers who may be troubled and, as a control, a second who are fairly normal. He takes them out on boats with cabins for a week. They can't bring screens or have showers but they do swim in the sea every day and work together to do essential chores to keep the vessel shipshape. The seas can be rough and the chores demanding, even frightening. The result is compelling. After even a few days the boys bond into a team, relish the challenge and adapt to the rigours beyond what you'd expect for such untested or depressed youngsters. As every class sports team or boot camp of army recruits has also found, young bloods can be whipped into shape quickly and thoroughly.

But they can also become terrorists and thugs. This is pliable material. And the sad lesson of recent years is that it is pitifully easy for Jet or any armed twerp to cause havoc and become world famous in seconds. Take a machine gun to a kindergarten (everyone seems to have a machine gun in America) and kill toddlers; drive a vehicle superfast through strolling pedestrians, murdering them in no time; use box cutters to capture planes and slam them into buildings; attack girls you don't know and become the Ripper of your local town. 'Tonight, I'll be on the national news,' said the Melbourne wastrel in January. He was going to be *somebody*. And he was right.

The lesson is plain. If you allow civil society to disintegrate (*'there is no such thing as society'*), you will pay for it. And the cost will be far more than the outlay that would have helped prevent these social catastrophes: social services, public facilities, places where people can enjoy themselves constructively outside the home. Employment.

And if Jet does become a recruit for the forces of darkness, treat him like the criminal he is, not as a warrior or a soldier in an enemy force. This is the advice of Masha Gessen, who wrote a book about the two Boston bombers. The brothers had been disaffected by their Chechen heritage and their directionless lives and it took little to make them into fanatics with a purpose. But the result of their bombing of marathon runners and spectators (the victims are immaterial to the perpetrators, as long as the deaths are shocking) was world attention and an assumption of some higher (evil?) purpose.

Once more immature men had made us feel that our entire world had become poisoned, even though everyone we know personally is civilised, kind and trying to live a constructive life. Well, nearly everyone. It takes barely a room full of driven young men to make us all think we've gone to Hell.

Could I have become Jet? Taken the path of Evil? Following is an article I wrote in 2003 at the time the Iraq war was being mooted. I was trying to fathom how I had turned away from juvenile violence to a completely different view — and whether it made sense. The *Sydney Morning Herald* called it 'Anger Management'. I'm not sure it was the right headline. See what you think.

*

I waited for Green after school. We were strong on surnames then. I don't recall ever knowing his first name.

Already there was a crowd. Other boys had heard I was going to beat him up. They stood about awkwardly, trying to hide their gloating anticipation. I saw Green walking out slowly with a couple of small friends in support. He gave me the weak smile of the hopeless. I said something pompous about a torn blazer, as if offering some Jesuitical excuse to a sceptical jury, then hit him hard in the face. He turned without resistance and so I pummelled his kidneys as if to break his back, simulating a cold frenzy.

This began to frighten my audience. They intervened at last, saying that Green had had enough. By now he was collapsed and coughing. His two friends looked on in despair and did nothing. I allowed myself to be restrained.

The following day, it was clear my efforts had been a success. I was famous within my 1950s London state-grammar school, and all the other 15 year olds, with the exception of Master Green, thought I was one hell of a lad. The fact my victim was as pugilistic as Bambi (and looked like him) mattered not at all. My feigned fury had registered: I was someone to be reckoned with. A Hard Man.

At the time, oddly enough, my smart friends and I were beginning to go on peace marches, wearing our crow's foot badges in the cause of banning the bomb and achieving world peace. Being a playground thug wasn't seen as contradictory. We learned our Stalinism young.

Adolescents may be excused, just, for mindful cruelty. Mine was entirely vainglorious and served briefly to bolster my sundry anxieties about growing up. The surprise was that violence was so easy and swift. Much more surprising was the readiness of both boys and teachers to accept its place in the achievement of destiny.

This shocked me. I knew boys would accept fighting as cool but I had no idea grown-ups could do so as well. I didn't apologise to my miserable, crushed victim, who may, to this day carry some psychological bruising. But I did, in my sudden hot shame, determine never to do anything like it again.

I changed my personal culture. In the process,

I rejected my upbringing in a household riven with violence and a Gradgrindian father who used stair rods instead of canes, and a fist if he was caught short and rods were out of reach. I never raised my hand to my children (my voice, perhaps) or to any person since. This much I owe to Green.

John Keegan, in his *A History of Warfare*, avers that conflict of the kind that blighted the twentieth century can be overcome only with a change of culture. It is not enough to refine the status quo. If anything can be inferred from the marches that preceded the latest war in Iraq, it is that such a change of culture might be upon us.

So many people, so many marches. The largest turnout ever seen in England, untold thousands in Australia. Many, many around the world. Serious folk who were surely not expecting George W Bush or John Howard to turn their troops homewards simply because their democracies were demonstrating noisy opposition. Some strident rabblerousers marched and, OK, some of the usual suspects, but so did very many more of the broadcast range of all our societies. What they were asking for was a different way to solve international problems.

Our culture has been changed, paradoxically, because we are children of a violent age, steeped in the graphic portrayal of conflict. War for us is the gore and vomit of *Saving Private Ryan*, the arbitrary obliteration and loss of *Band of Brothers*, the inescapable growing dread of *The Pianist*. We have war to dinner. We are the first generation to do so since conflict was industrialised.

Now we want something else.

Another difficulty with war, apart from its almost farcical lottery, is how much it is accepted as a precise tool, as if lancing a boil. I have long seen it, instead, as a cancer. Cut it and it spreads, sending little metastases to the most unexpected places, where they wait, emerging as Bin Ladens or Saddams, Bosnias or Rwandas, years later.

Others have said the same. Les Carlyon, writing in *The Bulletin* about Gallipoli, said: 'Little wars, much like tumours, sometimes turn into big wars, not because those in charge intend this to happen, but because the thing they have created develops a life of its own. It grows on them, muddling their senses ...'

Yes, but I see the cancer of violence as more than that. It represents a kind of cellular anarchy — overwhelmingly a moral chaos. Will I attack the pack of thugs who threaten my daughter with rape? Or will I piously proclaim my peaceful persuasions and hope they politely turn and go? Will I agree with historian Geoffrey Blainey that the arithmetic of ghastliness is in favour of invading Iraq when you compare the hundreds of thousands of innocents destroyed if Saddam is left in place? Or will I refuse to do numerical body counts? Is it better to pulverise a thousand ordinary families (called collateral damage) or half a million through state terror?

That is the moral chaos of *Sophie's Choice*.

Which of your children would you prefer be annihilated? Choose. The little boy? Or the younger little girl? Choose and be co-opted by the evil. Complicit.

Our challenge now is to prevent the absurdity, the threat of rape, the drums of war, arising in the first place.

In a violent situation it hardly matters what you do. You are mired in a moral absurdity. If you are big and strong like Rambo and carrying a laser-guided state-of-the-art superweapon, then no doubt you can vanquish the hoodlums and save your daughter. Or, if you have a codicil to a peace treaty (weapons of mass destruction) and you can claim it has been disobeyed (and you're big and strong like Rambo and have superweapons), you can invade and topple Saddam.

But what if you don't? What if you face the rapists weak and empty-handed? What if you have no Kuwait-inspired codicil?

In February [2003] I met Harvard professor John Holdren straight off the plane from Beijing. The Chinese, he said, were mystified. 'Why are you invading Iraq?' they had whispered, strictly off the record. 'And why are you *not* invading North Korea?'

'Because we can,' replied Holdren. 'If we did to Pyongyang what we intend to do to Baghdad, Kim Jong-il would have nuclear rockets descending on Seoul before you can whistle Dixie.'

Iraq was a rare free kick. Most other nations aren't such lone mongrels. They have alliances far more forbidding than Saddam could pretend. But

even the straightforward biffing Iraq received
(as easy as my tussle with Green) has had plenty
of chaotic consequences. Immediately: looting,
catastrophic losses, the rise of a mafia and religious
zealotry. In the long term: the lifelong resentment
of those bereaved, new terrorists and political
quagmire.

Could the Americans and their 'willing' friends
do something similar again? Unlikely. Not only
because Iraq is a one-off, but because most wars
from now will not be our side versus theirs. They
will either be civil wars or international policing. On
these criteria, interestingly, this last excursion to Iraq
could easily be justified, for it was far from being a
sovereign nation at peace.

*

One of the legacies of the Cold War has been the
number of brutal tyrants placed in charge by or
supported by the West in countries at risk of a leftist
takeover. In the Congo (formerly Zaire), Chile, El
Salvador, Afghanistan, the Philippines, Vietnam and
Iraq, our own thug was set up to keep out their thug.
Massive supplies of weaponry were usually provided.

The result was usually an unending internal war.
I'll call it a friendly war in the same jaundiced spirit
as we refer to friendly fire: getting zapped by our
own side by mistake. Friendly warfare involves all
the terror Saddam imposed: torture, arbitrary arrest,

the plunder of supplies, the fascist state.

The question is whether we have an obligation to terminate such friendly war regimes for which our side bears some significant responsibility. I would suggest we do. If diplomatic means do not work, invasion is the only alternative.

But it must be by a force capable of imposing change. A UN-backed effort is preferable, but it should be more than a handful of soldiers in blue hats standing around wringing their hands. (One wonders, in this context, what 1400 French-led troops will manage in the Congo, where so far an estimated 3.1 million to 4.7 million have died in the civil war.) Such 'policing' must include repair and reconstruction as required by the 'liberated'.

According to a remarkable survey by *The Economist*, 'almost all wars are now civil wars'. The set-piece war between groups of allies could well be left in the twentieth century.

This makes sense. Most rich countries are irrevocably intertwined with each other by trading deals and exchanges of citizenry as tourists, academics or business. The consequences of a rift would be unthinkable even between old foes such as China and the US. Poor countries under colonial regimes, says *The Economist*, had their tribal factions kept largely under control. The gradual removal of imperial government unleashed these unresolved differences. This has been the worst in multi-ethnic societies where one group forms a large majority.

Poverty is almost always a common factor in

this process. So, I would assume, is the absence of an effective democracy. I can think of hardly any wars where each side is democratic.

Back to poverty. 'Why are poor, stagnant countries so vulnerable?' asks *The Economist*. 'Partly because it is easy to give a poor man a cause. But also, almost certainly, because poverty and low or negative growth are often symptoms of corrupt, incompetent government, which can provoke rebellion. They are also common in immature societies, whose people have not figured out how to live together.'

What's also common is the resort to arms. Such countries spend an average of nearly 5 per cent of GDP on the military, impoverishing the rest of society and making uprisings more likely.

The answer, according to *The Economist*, is spending on health and education, which quickly demonstrates a real hope of progress and makes an immediate difference to people's lives.

What does all this mean in policy terms for countries like Australia? There are four main points.

First, it requires us to engage more thoroughly in our region. Australia's reputation is dire in Asia, the very place where our future relationships are so important. Ex-diplomat and writer Alison Broinowski told the *Sydney Morning Herald*, 'Australia is seen as a second-rate western country still tainted by the memories of the White Australia policy, lacking culture and history, inept in negotiation and image promotion — large, lucky and lazy.' Peacemakers need to be open to the subtleties of other cultures, willing to listen, be patient and offer real help. The reward is stability in the region and inoculation against Bin Ladens.

Second, we need a stricter definition of our role in any international police force. We have an obligation, having provoked them, to intervene in friendly wars. We have already done this in Afghanistan, East Timor and Iraq. But the diplomatic shambles before the latter involvement cannot be repeated. We have seen that, if an internationally agreed effort is not mounted, then the USA will go it alone. This is unacceptable. We must deploy an effective agreement that most nations will support. The only answer to the USA is the rest of the world combined. Then the USA must join in.

It will be hard. But there is no alternative — except the USA as the Lone Ranger. And Australia must stop playing Tonto.

Third, it demands a thorough examination of those factors likely to cause conflicts. Most wars are now civil (a term almost as repugnant as 'friendly') and have identifiable causes. In the future, environmental forces will make these worse. A flooded Bangladesh, vanquished by global warming, could have 140 million refugees looking for somewhere to live. Water, tempest, newly minted diseases: stand by for a turbulent century. Science, properly supported and international in outlook, will be crucial.

Fourth, an arms trade which has grown to obscene proportions must be severely restricted.

We have to stop arming potential enemies. We save
in the long run. And I don't mean only Saddams,
Bin Ladens and Afghan warlords. Charlton Heston
is wrong: guns do kill. Spread them about and they
will create the chaos of war.

And let's stop pretending there are good wars.
War means mistakes, crippled babies, violated women
and death. All wars. They are organised chaos.
Always will be.

Thomas Hobbes, that largely unappreciated
vanguard of the Enlightenment, saw most of
this some 360 years ago. In *Leviathan* (1651),
he identified self-interest as a prime mover for
peacemakers. He also foresaw the role of an
international enforcer. As John Gray, Professor
of European Thought at the London School of
Economics, writes:

> Hobbes favoured international cooperation to reduce
> the causes of conflict … The causes of conflict can be
> understood, and human behaviour improved.
>
> By understanding why humans act as they do,
> rulers could secure what Hobbes called 'commodious
> living' — a condition of thriving arts, sciences and
> industry, in which human passions are no longer a
> source of destructive conflict.

This, it seems to me, is the essence of the
overwhelming public display we saw in the
demonstrations around the world in response
to the threat of war in Iraq in 2003. It was not

the expression of a confused left or a parade of misguided idealism. Not a plea, I would argue, for peace at all costs, but one for a different way of doing things. Even soldiers, who should know, have realised the limits of armed force.

So, we should see our era as one of transition. If, as Hobbes proposed, we are to help a majority attain 'commodious living', then quite a few of the remaining cancers spread from previous conflicts have to be identified and treated. The infamous events of September 11 make that process especially urgent. Too many murderous villains are secreted in the crevices of civilisation prepared to unleash Armageddon. But the very willingness to carry out the policing must contain a determination to make it redundant and obsolete. Can the UN become effective enough to manage such a task?

Nations, like teenage boys, must mature. There is nothing sophisticated about violence, however space-age the weaponry. There is nothing heroic about sending sons to places unknown to kill folk they've never met, for reasons they don't comprehend. Armies may be valiant; they are also harbingers of deep trauma. We now know this.

It is time our policies changed accordingly. Otherwise we shall become inward-looking societies in a permanent state of siege. Otherwise we shall simply have to take out our babies and line them up to be killed before taking our turn to do likewise to the enemy.

Otherwise we shall inherit a whirlwind. As

Rudyard Kipling wrote in memory of his soldier son, killed in World War I:

If any question why we died,
Tell them, because our fathers lied.

*

That was written 15 years ago. The costs of those wars, Iraq and Afghanistan, have been far greater than I or any of us imagined possible in 2003. George W and Tony Blair thought it would be a quick *whack*, the collapse of a noisy foreigner followed by dancing in the street. It is still going on: millions dead, cities devastated, the worst refugee crisis since World War II and a cost of so many trillions in any currency you care to nominate. And arms sales, even from Australia, rival people smuggling and drugs as global export trades. The metastases have spread everywhere.

Could it have been different, as my essay proposed? Indeed, it could. What you need is the kind of culture change historian Keegan talked about. My own personal culture changed. I made a choice. The background was experience of a ruined central Europe, refugees under the bed (Trudi's sister) and parents who fought with all the physical violence of a pub brawl.

Some, such as Professor Steve Pinker, claim we have, most of us, changed our culture and our world has far less violence. But Pinker is not willing to recognise what some have called the black swans of this argument:

the 'evil' wild cards that spring from chaos, from choreographed aggression (such as the boys' bold shirtfronting Trump and Kim indulge in) to the threat of rampaging climate change. These sudden eruptions, though not unexpected, can unleash catastrophe. That would be real evil, because it would be hopeless.

We need experienced diplomats who know their history. We don't need bully boys waving their rockets. We need people determined to maintain a civil society and who know, pace Thatcher, what society is made of. We need great leadership. We do not have it now.

Hatred

I am usually in deep loathing of someone in the ABC and it's usually someone in charge. Now you'd imagine that a crock like me who's reached beyond maturity to a great age, an age even greater than my father, who has been dead for 56 years — I am 74, he died at 57 — should be more mellow, accepting of authority, quietly realistic. But no. The world has changed.

Institutions have changed most of all. Many of us have never felt so powerless. We are governed by email and required to perform online contortions that are supposed to make us feel engaged. We are consulted during rushed meetings when we are essentially handed the latest instructions and can merely ask clarifying questions about our fate, like immigrants emerging from the hold of a bleak ship being told the rules of their new land. I am told that this is the same throughout large organisations, but I wouldn't know.

Compare the days when that supposed tyrant (basically a big teddy bear) David Hill was in charge. If he heard through his remarkable network (eyes and ears everywhere) that some of us had won another prize or scored ratings beyond belief, the phone would ring and there he'd be in person announcing he had champagne and some tinnies in the fridge upstairs and would we care to nip up and join him in a toast.

At Christmas we'd be invited to his huge garden near the racetrack in Randwick where a vast barbecue would be laid on and opera singers mixed with football players and ABC staff and a few arias provided the crescendo of a charming and highly original evening. Nowadays there is basic drink out on the office terrace combined with memos about responsible consumption of grog during office hours. I (loudly) augment such official warning by requesting that we also make our adultery 'responsible' when on site. Most gatherings are farewell parties.

Like David Hill, Ken Myer was similarly informal and generous. This tall scion of the great megastore family was a mature captain of industry when I first met him, just before he became chairman of the ABC board. Running the ABC and leading major reform you'd expect him to be elusive. He was the first chair when the ABC turned from being a public service commission into an independent corporation in 1983.

Back then I did *The Science Show* live on Saturdays. The following Monday morning Ken would be on the phone telling me, in a friendly collegial way, what he'd liked and what he had not. He often found David Suzuki OTT — too negatively predictable. Sometimes Ken would drop in to our staff meetings, just for a chat. He'd rarely show signs of wanting to leave and his tiny wife, Yasuko, would have to give him tiny nudges. Ken would still hold forth, until dragged away. We loved it.

*

Over 60 years ago the demon of my teenage dreams was the headmaster WH Hore. Yes, Colonel Hore had parents who did not notice that their son's name looked like a hooker's shingle. Colonel Hore and I clashed from the beginning. Not because I failed academically (in fact I usually came top in his geography classes), but because I hated being in the cadet corps, which he treasured, and he hated my wearing ban-the-bomb badges, which he deemed against the rules. On reflection, Freddy, as he liked to be called in later years, was a traditional schoolmaster who had the interests of his working-class pupils at heart. He wanted us to get to Oxbridge and succeed as postwar grammar-school boys and girls were supposed to do. (I was deemed unsuitable, as explained in an earlier chapter.) For him, rules, standards, even those carried by army uniforms on teenage bodies, were all part of the enlightened process.

He used to remind me of a younger Prince Philip in style and demeanour. He was handsome in a conventional British way, decisive, yet, as he admitted later, performing the role he thought was expected, like an actor. He never appeared in any kind of military uniform at school and spoke, unlike Prince Philip, with a West Country inflexion. It turns out I may have had a false schoolboy view of him as a Dickensian Gradgrind, as I realised much later.

I wrote about Colonel Hore in my memoirs, *And Now For Something Completely Different*, 35 years ago. He was given a copy and found my depiction of his authoritarian side disconcerting. But that was nothing compared to the splenetic letter my brother wrote to his old headmaster — we'd both been to Bec School, where Colonel Hore presided, and from which Shwn Williams had been expelled for similarly, but more intransigently, disobeying the rules. I can't recall his exact misdemeanours but I am sure it was a case of unredeemable loathing of the institution and all it stood for.

My brother looked like his hero, my father: the same lean grace and handsome oval face with straight hair, unlike my curly mop. Shwn also had Gwyn's practical flair and could repair anything, almost as quickly as I could break it. He could fathom machines just by looking at them and often made me doubt we could be brothers, our abilities were so different.

Shwn became an academic in France, lecturing in languages at the University of Nantes, and by the early 1990s you'd have thought he'd be well over the snarling hatreds of youth. Not so. Just look at this sample of what he wrote to poor Freddy:

Tooting Bec Grammar was particularly noteworthy as a place where grown men inflicted their apparent inability to relate to other human beings on little boys forced to wear short trousers and silly uniforms. Having rather uninteresting people strutting around in self-importance with the open encouragement and authority to destroy any displays of self-respect, curiosity of mind or youthful spirit (for the good of one-and-all) is extremely reminiscent of the Nazis or of any other perverted mental thought process.

Being a nasty piece of work to gain recognition was indeed the ethos of the school. And all the drilling and veneer of Anglicanism, which had as much to do with metaphysics as playing marbles, and you already have all the trappings of fascism.

My brother was over 40 when he wrote the above tirade, plus another three dense pages.

Freddy, at great length, replied to me, not to my incandescent brother:

I enclose an account of my wartime activities. I was one of the lucky ones — I survived but a lot of my friends did not. The Selwyn College [Cambridge] war memorial contains the names of at least a dozen friends.

Most pupils fall into the trap of thinking they know all about the school and know how much better they would run it. In fact, they have little knowledge and I would like to have the opportunity over a pint to fill you in. You may have a surprise or two. The other mistake is what they think of their headmaster. The art of head-mastering contains quite an element of acting and pupils are often surprised subsequently to discover what they thought was an old ogre is in fact a broadminded, civilised human being with a strong basic sense of humour whose sole concerns are for the individual benefit of each pupil and the welfare of the school in equal proportion.

I was rather sorry for the old fellow, now retired south of London. I went to see him and we chatted in a ritualistic way. He, as befitted a Mr Chips of the latter half of the twentieth century, took credit for all our successes, despite having dismissed us as hopeless when young. I had transmogrified from a failure to a puzzling achiever. And I could see his grudging willingness to reassign me swiftly to the glory list. I was also tickled to hear that he used to hide whenever he heard my mother was on the phone or worse (in the early days when not housebound) *on her way*. Ray had no fear of panjandra and, indeed, when we were in Vienna, on finding an Austrian or German guest trying to defend Hitler along the lines of: '*He made mistakes but some of what he did was good ...*' she would throw them out, down the stone stairs.

The real transformation, however, came when I was elected a visiting fellow of Balliol. One day, after I was well settled in what is claimed to be Oxford's oldest college, I had a whim, something I thought would be a bit of a giggle rather than a grand gesture. I invited Colonel Hore to lunch in the Senior Common Room. This would be better than dining at High Table, which often took ages. Lunch was a sprint in and out as busy dons came from lectures and sped off to labs or tutorials.

I picked him up at the station and took him on a walk through some glorious sites he would enjoy. As we strolled past Geography, I spotted Professor Andrew Goudie and introduced my old headmaster. Give Freddy his due: he knew immediately of Goudie's work and background and conversed freely. After the tour we settled for lunch. The dons knew, of course, how to butter up an aged teacher, and you could see the old chap glowing in the attention. We had tea in the Common Room as academics disappeared.

Then back to the station. Of Shwn he said nothing. It was a pleasant resolution of an ancient feud, one of the lessons of life. I doubt that my brother would have approved, he was unswerving in his dislikes. But I have always felt it's useful to stem those ancient rages before they consume the present. It was the same experience with my domestic rearrangement way back, when the emotional chaos of raging antagonism changed, as a result of patient effort, into friendliness, even love. My former wife of 32 years is one of my closest friends, as is her husband, the conductor and composer Christopher Bowen. We see each other a lot and I enjoy their enormous contributions to music and the arts and they are among my most constant listeners.

Freddy was a silly old git who once seemed the essence of establishment authority but with hindsight looks like an old-fashioned gent. He is now dead but before he went I sent him my letter from PM John Howard, who had given me a centenary medal. I thought Freddy's archive was the best place for it and I proved correct. A euphoric handwritten note was the last I heard from him. As an old Tory it chuffed him no end that a yobbo like me should get a missive from John Howard. My brother's hatred died with him; Shwn followed family tradition and went young at 60. He was not the forgiving type, and suffered accordingly.

*

Two people I have known stand out as being, apparently, incapable of hatred. One was Patricia Goldacre, the other Professor Peter Mason.

Pat was the granddaughter of Sir Henry Parkes, herself a teacher but trained in psychology, which she applied to distressed children. She grew up in Sydney and then moved to Oxford, then south London, where I met her through her son, Michael, my school chum. She was one of those instrumental in establishing the Campaign for Nuclear Disarmament and spoke about it at the United Nations in company with Lord Boyd Orr, scientist and Nobel laureate.

Hers was a combination now rare: Christian sensibilities, though secular, with socialist principles. However cross she was about political viciousness or personal venom, she never categorised the perpetrators as hopeless villains. Pat's arguments never stooped to pull out the Nazi card. She seemed a natural manifestation of that instinct, nurtured through learning and lifelong practice, of rejecting evil as an easy label. The Devil had no role in Pat's long life. She was a natural peacemaker, whatever the awfulness she had to deal with.

I remember her in the depths of a raging crowd in the middle of Grosvenor Square in 1968 as police on horses charged towards us during a demo against the Vietnam War. She suddenly screamed in apparent abject fear, a real yell — and the cops backed off. As they went she grinned conspiratorially at us, her hand hiding her face from Sergeant Plod. She'd been pretending, and it worked.

Michael, her son, is now Professor Emeritus in Public Health at Oxford. Pat's grandson Ben is a famous science writer and stirrer. When Ben comes to Australia on a speaking tour and tells folk that he's the great-great-grandson of Sir Henry Parkes, they often reply, 'Yeah, the old rake — hundreds around here make that claim too, mate.' It was a lusty family.

A mark of Pat's Bloomsbury enlightenment in both learning and lovers was the way previous boyfriends, even including her former husband, Michael Goldacre's father, Reg, were assigned room on every floor of her tall house in Balham. At one point four exes were positioned up the staircase and I imagined the house growing taller as her romances burgeoned. She kept this bohemian existence going while displaying all the charm and sweetness of a regal vestal virgin.

Peter Mason's well of goodwill was more tragic in origin.

On 6 March 2017, I and the vice-chancellor of Macquarie University gathered with a splendour of professors (I am assured that's the collective noun) in the lecture theatre (E6?) where exactly 50 years before Peter Mason had given the first-ever lecture at the new institution of higher education. He'd talked about the physics of materials, a topic he knew much about, having done research at the CSIRO and before that in London.

I spoke about my encounters with Peter, who died tragically in 1987, as he became first a passable and then a brilliant broadcaster. He started with a simple book review, read in a singsong voice, a few clichés cluttering the prose, and I gave him notes. It was duly broadcast. The following week he arrived with another talk which showed all my notes had been absorbed and he was twice as good.

The graph of his improvement then became nigh vertical. Next, he turned up with a script of many pages and I started to worry. It was on the history of navigation and called 'Genesis to Jupiter'. Why not the history of the pencil or green wellies? What made this nice man imagine the public wanted to listen to hours on radio about maps and finding your way to strange places? It required actors, singers, original music and, I muttered after he left: 'No doubt some jugglers, plus a few elephants and the Berlin Philharmonic.'

I decided to record it swiftly and bury it in the summer season. This we did. And the fan mail began, immediately, to arrive in crates. A publisher demanded the rights for a book, duly published in 1978. What was happening? Peter had become a star. We were dumbfounded. His secret was twofold: storytelling plus a firm belief in science for the people. His optimism about the human condition was profound but backed up by deep knowledge, well displayed in his scripts. He followed navigation with series on light, on rubber, blood and iron, bikes, and on and on — each taking a line through another prosaic topic and turning it into an adventure about the way history, science and the common creative spirit has done so much for the lives of everyone.

In 'Blood and Iron' he juxtaposed the life-giving qualities of the ferrous molecule in our red blood cells (it's copper in arthropods such as lobsters, whose blood is therefore blue) as opposed to iron in guns and bullets and the materiel of war. He ranged from human physiology and medicine to human slavery and Krupp and asked for, and got, a specially composed electronic version of Wagnerian tunes to accompany the series. Another book followed the shows.

Then Peter was asked to reprise the first series, navigation, on stage in Melbourne for one of the final, and best, ANZAAS congresses in which science was brought to the people. (ANZAAS was the Australian and New Zealand Association for the Advancement of Science, which flourished for 109 years until amateurism and the old-boy network killed it off. It was the sister of the British Science Association of which Lisa Jardine and David Attenborough were once presidents.) We had an ark on stage with a demo of the dove being let fly by Noah — in Genesis — to rise high above the vessel to spot land on the horizon and fly in its direction, and the TV star Patrick Moore of BBC fame (*The Sky at Night*) told of *Voyager* flying to Jupiter and how far we'd come in navigating our way on land, sea and in the cosmos. From smart pigeons to spacecraft.

Peter read his lines from the stage in his usual thin, warm voice. But he was unlike his usual exuberant self. The neat hair was in place and he tried a few of his lovely smiles. But it wasn't the same ebullient Prof Mason I had known for so long.

The following day Peter told me he'd forgotten his phone number. Overnight this mathematical prodigy had become innumerate. A cancer in the left hemisphere of the brain had wiped away his numbers. Peter's answer, in a heartbreaking interview I subsequently broadcast on *The Science Show*, was cheerily to proclaim that now he'd have to concentrate on his right hemisphere and, after a lifetime of nerdy work using his left brain, he'd go arty using the other side.

I said all this at the 2017 Macquarie celebration at which the lecture theatre was renamed after Peter Mason. I told how he was willing to criticise the devils of history and of present-day antagonisms but how he did so with not a smidgin of venom or resentment. (So different from my brother's persistent bile.) Then I told of Peter's personal history, a man of the left, certainly, but one born of tolerance and pacifism.

Next came the shock. I spoke of something that it turned out no one in that packed hall had known. It was on that very day 100 years before that Peter Mason's grandmother Alice Wheeldon and his father Alf Mason had been put on trial, accused of plotting the murder of the British PM David Lloyd George. Alice had been a conscientious objector during World War I and had given sanctuary to draft avoiders, and it was said that the Secret Service had decided to set them up as plotters to poison the PM. Toxic drugs, supposedly obtained by Alf to kill guard dogs, were seized, and the story twisted to point to assassination.

Alice had suffered badly in prison and, despite being released by order of Lloyd George himself, had died two years later, her health ruined. On the Friday following the 2017 Macquarie celebration, protestors gathered outside the Law Courts in London loudly proclaiming Alice's innocence and demanding pardons for Alice and Alf.

Peter Mason never mentioned a word of this to me or anyone I knew (apart from his children, who told me only recently) and showed not one breath of hatred towards anyone. Yet, certainly compared to my brother, who'd had not much more than a rough trot at an average school, Peter could have been justified in belching fire.

Hatred, and I note this without piety and in full knowledge of the pleasures of black indulgence, invariably consumes the hater. But I still want to murder that smug bastard in TV management.

Christopher Reeve was the best Superman imaginable. He was beyond handsome, athletic and filled the blue leotard and cape like a real legend. He also had an irony he brought to his acting that made his defence of the American Way a real hoot instead of an embarrassment. He had been at the Ivy League Cornell University, studying French as well as acting, followed by the Juilliard School, which accounted for some of his aplomb. At Juilliard he shared a room with Robin Williams.

Then, in 1995, he fell off his horse and became a paraplegic. Even his breathing had to be assisted by a machine. He turned to science and stem cell research and became quite erudite about it all. The then premier of New South Wales, Bob Carr, heard about this and invited Reeve to Sydney to promote the science in the face of objections from fundamentalists who were bothered by concepts of scientists 'playing God' and fiddling with germ lines, the essence of 'life'.

Carr called a press conference. Superman lay immobile on a trolley before us. His face was unmistakable and his circumstance shocking. As a result, none of the gathered press, normally shameless and feral, could muster a question.

So I put up my hand and said, conversationally: 'Christopher Reeve, welcome. My name, and this is not a joke, is Robyn Williams. Could you tell us how easy it's been to master the complexities of neuroscience and stem cells?'

Reeve began to laugh — not easy when you're paralysed. 'Well, thanks,' he said. 'I'd like to tell you that, when I had my accident I was willing to kill myself, somehow, but then your namesake came to my bedside. He's a dear friend. He told me jokes for two days and showed me life is still worth living. So, I'm here.' All this with the assistance of a machine helping him to breathe. And then he spoke science.

The next day, at Government House by the harbour, I and one other were allowed to talk to him privately in one of the reception rooms. I held his hand (it seemed appropriate) and we talked about the opposition to the neurological R&D. Even with this research, with its enormous promise, there is ideological turmoil. Outside, in front of a crowd of notables in the exquisite gardens, Superman gave a talk on nerve physiology and its applications, as clear and informed as anyone I've heard anywhere. Soon we were oblivious to his breathing machine and how he had to speak in delayed, staccato sentences, measuring his observations with the same deliberation and economy as Stephen Hawking has done, with similar unthinkable restrictions. We were astounded.

Twenty years later at UCLA I was with the team who had tried to help Christopher Reeve to walk again. Reggie Edgerton and friends had found ways to 're-educate' the lower part of the severed spinal cord, to reconnect it with information from the rest of the body about movement and interactions. Reeve had tried to walk on a treadmill, but he was too tall and became faint. He had to rest, then insisted on going again. He nearly managed a few steps. Any progress, he said, was so important. He would not give up.

'We found out some years ago that the spinal cord circuitry can learn,' Edgerton said. 'What's referred to as a complete spinal cord injury, that means no information can get down or up across that lesion, but people don't realise that the circuitry below that lesion is pretty much intact. It has forgotten a lot of stuff but it's still there. And so the bottom line is, if we can figure out a way to reengage the circuitry, then it can relearn how to walk and to stand and do the things that it would normally do.'

Today, the progress is formidable. Patients may need an 'exoskeleton' over their legs to provide support, but one chap, previously paralysed, has now walked for four years. Reggie and co. stimulate the central nervous system below the break by means of an insertion like the epidural that delivers pain-killing drugs to women during childbirth. But the guys in LA, having done so much physiologically, want better technology. So, they are teaming up with UTS smack opposite where I work at the ABC in Ultimo. UTS will help provide engineering know-how.

'These findings are so new,' Edgerton assured me at UCLA, 'and in many ways unexpected, that it has told us that we are not even close to the limit. But the technical potential I would say is 20 years ahead of our clinical ability to take advantage of the technology. So, we've got to get them matched. The injured nervous system can do much more than what we anticipated.' As for the next step, he says, 'I always say at this stage right now we are at the Model T Ford stage, and we want to get to the Tesla.'

Superman, in spirit, returns once more to Sydney. This is the real meaning of 'elite'. Good-looking actors with marvellous brains and a depth of talents that always transcend any celebrity.

Christopher Reeve died in 2004 from what appeared to be an adverse reaction to antibiotics following sepsis. He was 52. The work he championed still goes on. The latest, surprising advance is the use of carbon fibres, thin and strong as well as resistant to rejection, being used to 'rewire' parts of the central nervous system. Clinical trials are underway in Michigan and other parts of the US.

*

Richard Dawkins' *The Selfish Gene* was published just over 40 years ago. I interviewed Richard via satellite at the time (1976) and was surprised by his boyish voice and clarity of thought. I wasn't sure I understood the central point of the book but it was packed with brilliant ideas and thrilling imagery. Richard had been influenced by the modest but inspiring Bill Hamilton, who had worked out why we tend to favour our own group or family: altruism depends on close genetic relationships. *The Selfish Gene* explained how stable populations can evolve and diminish the role of the individual organism in the process. Hence the divide between Richard and

Stephen Jay Gould, who insisted that it is the whole creature that competes and survives, not just its chromosomes and populations. It is worth reading Richard's book *Brief Candle in the Dark* for a neat summary of his 'selfish' idea.

One thing was certain: he was talking about selfish *genes*, not a selfish society. This was no Darwinian encomium for carnivorous capitalism, no social allegory. Richard is as soggy as a left-leaning, *Guardian*-reading egalitarian, as are many of his critics.

Over the next 40 years he kept writing at a formidable rate, always displaying a vast range of reading in the classics from Chaucer to Shakespeare and beyond. Richard, like fellow withering critic of God, the late Christopher Hitchens, is a typical graduate of Balliol College: 'Effortlessly Superior'.

His reputation, though, is mixed. At one point he was voted Britain's leading intellectual. But many journalists delight in saying horrid things about his irascibility and even arrogance. He is an easy mark for professional hit-hacks, the columnists who have too many paragraphs to fill and do so with feigned venom.

For me, and I write this as a friend and one-time babysitter for Richard (would you believe he has preserved the note his daughter wrote on the night in 1996 claiming my friend who came to visit while I was babysitting had scoffed her dinner?), his failings are twofold and mild: he has been in Oxford too long and, above all, he needs to stop tweeting. Or, at least, wait 20 minutes before pressing *send* to his 2.8 million Twitter followers.

I don't tweet, but I know the syndrome. You see a comment from someone that ignites instant rage; you write two quick coruscating sentences and go *click* despite the late hour. I have managed to call a couple of senior ABC managers 'vermin' (inspired by Welsh political genius Aneurin Bevan who described the Tories in this way) and I have questioned the parentage of other colleagues in email messages written before second thoughts have intruded. It is important to remember, Richard, that this kind of mail is there forever, like words in a book. The sheer brevity adds a pitiless unadorned impact. He is hurt by the inference that he is being acerbic. He thinks he's being plain. Richard does not mind exposing and badmouthing the trolls, but he hates discovering that nice people think badly of him.

Richard tweets at frenzied rates like Trump or the late Mark Colvin, and this can allow a tone quite unlike that of his normal discourse or considered thoughts on the page. Just read his latest books. There he describes his relaxed and friendly relationships with vicars and bishops, his willingness as a senior don to say grace in Hall before dinner (he has no objection to saying 'meaningless' words, only lying ones) and enjoyment of friendly argument. He is also easily brought to tears by nature, by poetry, by art and music and by Balliol.

Too long in Oxford? Many of my friends, like Richard, have been there for over 50 years. They are schooled in critical thinking — or annoying nit-picking if you prefer. This habit manifests itself in replying to any comment with a pompous look up at the ceiling and pronouncing ever so slowly: 'Well, it depends on what you mean by *the*.' You reply that everyone knows the meaning of *the* — it is the main point I'm trying to get over, not a redefinition of all the terms in my last sentence.

This last sin is not one Richard is guilty of very often but it erupts now and then. One of the nasty experiences that made him more suspicious, less trusting of strangers, and especially of TV crews, was being ambushed by some film people from Australia who came to his home. They could have been creationists in disguise and he writes of this in *Brief Candle* so I won't explore it here. But constant attacks have made him sometimes regret his profile.

In the early days I used to visit Richard in his Mansfield Road flat near the Oxford labs where we recorded many an interview, sometimes in company with his wife Lalla Ward, the actor and artist. She was in *Doctor Who* and enjoyed the company of then Doctor Tom Baker. Richard had sent a fan letter to Douglas Adams after the broadcasts of *Hitchhiker's Guide to the Galaxy* and an episode of *Doctor Who* and Adams invited him to a party. Lalla was there. They married and later moved to their house in North Oxford where her exuberant sense of fun is displayed in the contents of the rooms — including the horses and other menagerie from merry-go-rounds, visible from the street through the house's big bay windows. Richard and Lalla are fun and far from the morose scolds of tabloid legend — though how this has changed since their separation in 2016 combined with continued cohabitation in that lovely home one can't say. I'm told they are as friendly as ever, on different floors, with the occasional lunch. They seemed happy as ever in September 2017, laughing in the garden.

In 2006, when Richard was about to publish *The God Delusion*, I was staying opposite his present college, New (which, typically of Oxford, is very old). On the day after I arrived from Australia he dropped the proofs of the book over by bike even before I got up. I spent the morning reading furiously. Then I went over for lunch by their indoor swimming pool and to record an interview. I promised to hold the result for broadcast until publication. *Delusion* works steadily through the ways in which science demolishes the evidence for God. It goes through contradictions in the Bible and other religious literature, and makes much of the cruel admonitions in, especially, the Old Testament in which horrendous punishments are required for errant behaviour. Being stoned to death is a mild example.

I returned to my rooms, pleased as Punch with my scoop packed with purple patches — and found half of it was missing. The recorder, for the first time ever, had partially failed. There is nothing more disconcerting in broadcasting than the sudden realisation that something has *gone*. Irretrievably. What to do? I couldn't go back, there wasn't time. What about other Oxford recordings? All were fine. Why was only Richard's in bits? Was this God's revenge?

I went to London and visited our ABC office in Portland Place (long since closed). We tested the device and I diagnosed a faulty flex connecting the mike to the recorder. I borrowed a new microphone and wire. It seemed to work. Clearly God knows how to sabotage flex.

What about Richard and *The God Delusion*? When I returned to Sydney I listened back to what was there of the 20-odd minutes I'd recorded. Gradually 34 years of editing experience took over. Where there were gaps I filled them with script and quotations from the book. Where paragraphs had connections, I joined them. We ended up with plenty to broadcast and the day was saved. Months later, at the Sydney Writers' Festival, I was on stage with Richard beamed in by satellite. Tickets had gone in minutes. We went happily over familiar ground. The audience laughed a great deal: atheism turned out to be fun. At the end I asked, 'What if the evidence, absent at the moment, for God's existence turned up? You are very keen on evidence! Would you chuck a U-ey?'

Richard smiled over the satellite. 'It's not very likely,' he grinned, cool about the argot, 'but, yes, I'd chuck a U-ey.'

Now he has second thoughts and can't imagine what that 'evidence' might be. He is recovering from his stroke, with only a hoarse voice and a slightly errant typing finger to worry about. His new book, of which he's written one chapter, is a version of *The God Delusion* for children. He's always been annoyed by kids being labelled as Catholic or Protestant or Muslim before they can walk, let alone think. He is keen to come to Australia again with his new (young) girlfriend. And he may even try to restrain those tweets. I hope so.

*

The last time I interviewed Sir David Attenborough I met him in the ABC foyer, gave him a big hug and said, 'Do you realise that we have done 100 years of science communication between us?'

Without missing even half a beat, he replied: 'That means you must have done 20!'

Never underestimate DA. Before an event or filming he is business-like, concise, even abrupt. When the time comes to record, chat, explore, he is at ease, forthcoming, controlled. It is one secret of his long, immensely productive life.

His brother Richard was an actor (*Jurassic Park*), and also a film producer and director of great distinction. He became a lord. The youngest brother, John, went into the motor trade. Though at the posh end of cars, I often wondered how he felt about being the third in a line-up of such talent and how he managed at parties when, having chatted about Dickie and David, he was asked, 'And what do *you* do?'

When I met David to do our first interview in 1979 about the series *Life on Earth*, he hadn't yet been sanctified by the viewing public. After his initial stint on BBC TV as a performer, he'd agreed to become a suit. He ran BBC2 and invented the long series with *Civilisation* (Kenneth Clark, 1969) and *The Ascent of Man* (Jacob Bronowski, 1973), both considered among the best programs ever made. Now he was about to present his own 13-part series about plants and animals all over the world. Its reputation preceded it both in critical acclaim and lavish expense.

I asked David about the money it cost and he replied that if you did something really well, tried hard to achieve what may appear to be impossible, said 'yes' to what-if questions (why not fly as high as we can, visit all seven continents, climb to the top of the tallest trees?), then everyone is keen to buy the series and you end up amortising the cost. It becomes no more expensive than ordinary documentaries. So why not do the best you can?

That has been the second professional secret of this incredible man since the beginning. Innovate and aim high. He started in television as a second choice when it was barely up and running in the 1950s. He was not quite good enough, he says, to make it into the more exclusive medium of radio! He has seen every new technique and run with it if, and only if, it has proved useful. Sixty years later he is still experimenting with 3D, CGI, filming from deep-diving subs, using all the paraphernalia, but at the same time making plain, correct language and big ideas (combined with vast enthusiasm) the essential currency of his craft. The best of the old with the best of the new. Don't abandon the simple human connection as you exploit the flashy gizmos.

David also has a commitment to service. You can hardly underestimate how many requests, how much mail, a man like this gets every day: the accumulated contacts of a very long lifetime, the thousands of viewers who write in, the lovers of nature who want some help with an endangered bird or rare plant. Yet he deals with the lot with grace and old-fashioned courtesy.

Two examples. A colleague of mine in radio, Gretchen Miller, wanted to interview David at his home in Richmond, London, in company with her young son, Keir, who happens to share the same birthday. Yes, came the reply and the pair duly arrived with a recorder and David, typically, answered the 12 year old's questions with all the patience and thoroughness he would offer to a Nobel laureate or *60 Minutes* star reporter.

Secondly, a neighbour asked whether I'd give David a note from her son about a didgeridoo from the Northern Territory. I duly passed it on in a folder during a crowded lunch at the Australian Museum as David was being inducted into their Hall of Fame and having a slug (a very pretty slug) named after him. I did not, in such circumstances, expect more than a glance at the piece of paper from the great man. I could say I'd done my neighbourly duty.

Two weeks later a neat envelope arrived in the post from England. It contained a handwritten letter from David in blue ink answering the didgeridoo questions, adding some points about traditional protocols, and giving his correspondent a thrill beyond measure. Both are examples of a great professional taking pains beyond mere obligation and doing so willingly. It's all or nothing. Most in our media trade just don't bother, the burden is too much of a nuisance. But, if you decide that everything other than press releases and spam is a proper human contact and you must deal with it and quickly, life becomes much more straightforward, and rewarding, though bloody busy. David Attenborough's understanding of this is an inspiration.

And in 2017, at the age of 91, he launched yet another gigantic series, *Blue Planet II*, made with all the control, idealism and basic decency that's lasted him nearly a century at the top of a field he helped invent.

I've often wondered what it was about that family from Leicester and the father who headed the local educational institute that became the university. There were brains in the family, so much is obvious, but also a sense of public service and responsibility. The interesting thing is that none of that Attenborough commitment looks the least bit out of date in 2018.

*

When I first met Lisa Jardine, founding director of the Centre for Interdisciplinary Research in the Humanities at the University College London and self-described 'loud-mouthed Jewess' in 2013, we had a row. Only a little one. It was about science reporting. She said it was being done badly. Too much clickbait (my term, not hers) about those never-ending Earth-like planets (only 40 light years away, we must go there!), those cures for the latest killer-plague, visiting American super techno-wizard promises of self-drive dildos — you've got the idea. I said there was another way and some of us do it. We ended up agreeing.

So, what did this president of the British Science Association and Booker Prize judge, this famous professor in two universities, this author of so many books, want us to think about, scientifically?

'History,' she replied, smiling a komodo smile.

'But isn't history so last century?' I teased.

She grinned like a pussycat this time, and we were friends.

We talked about her series on BBC Radio 4, *Seven Ages of Science*, that I wanted to broadcast. She was a professor of history and saw patterns in the spread of our times, and she could see how science comes not from random 'breakthroughs' but from the nature of the society it springs from — hence Jared Diamond's book *Guns, Germs and Steel*, showing why the industrial revolutions and growth of empires came from Europe and not from Papua New Guinea. We had guns and steel, they could not resist our germs. Society rules.

'My producer and I conceived of the seven ages of science as the age of ingenuity, the age of exploration, of opportunity, of inspiration, of the laboratory, of war and the age of *now*,' she told me as we sat in her study at University College London. Her blonde hair and lively, handsome features were those of a much younger woman and I was surprised to learn she was 69.

She carried the *Seven Ages* series like a star and took the ideas, literally, into the street, asking people about monuments they'd never really noticed and discoveries they'd only ever half-considered.

At that first meeting, with my recorder on, I went through her 'Ages of Science' and then hit her with this question, out of the blue: 'And your father was Jacob Bronowski. He is considered to be one of the greatest science broadcasters *ever*.' She nodded. 'You may like to know that one of his producers on *Ascent of Man* was my friend Dick Gilling, who's now living in Sydney and was co-creator of *Quantum*, predecessor of *Catalyst* on ABC TV.' She looked at me intensely and leaned forward very close.

I added, 'Dick told me *Ascent* was so arduous it helped shorten your father's life.'

She told me she remembered Dick well. I told her he lives in Sydney and his son Tom writes books and elegant reviews for Australian newspapers. By this time people were knocking on her door about her next engagement. She ignored them.

'Yes,' she said, 'it was a massive strain. But my father's commitment was absolute.'

She told me that Bruno (his nickname) did not want to do the renowned final piece to camera outside the gas chambers of Auschwitz but he agreed on the basis that, whatever happened, it would be done in one take with no script. They knew they had a series of spectacular quality on their hands and the BBC crew encouraged their famous star to have a go in what seemed to be potentially shattering circumstances. So out he came from the killing sheds and stood by the pond. As he slowly sank into the crumbling detritus soaking into his new shoes thinking about what to say, he realised that it was the bones of countless Jews under his feet, some perhaps relatives of his own family, lying in the grey waters lapping around his ankles. And he spoke these words:

This is the concentration camp and crematorium at Auschwitz. This is where people were turned into numbers. Into this pond were flushed the ashes of some 4 million people. And that was not done by gas. It was done by arrogance. It was done by dogma. It was done by ignorance. When people believe that they have absolute knowledge, with no test in reality, this is how they behave.

He paused, looked around, then back at the camera.

Science is a very human form of knowledge. We are always at the brink of the known; we always feel forward for what is to be hoped. Every judgement in science stands on the edge of error and is *personal*. Science is a tribute to what we can know although we are fallible. In the end, the words were said by Oliver Cromwell: 'I beseech you in the bowels of Christ: think it is possible you may be mistaken.'

He then turned and walked away from the camera. It is one of the most moving and powerful sequences in the history of television, not merely because of the setting, not so much because of the topic — done so many times before and since — but because Bruno was so utterly authentic, he was talking to you. He transcended the camera.

When we broadcast the interview with Lisa Jardine I added the actual soundtrack of Jacob Bronowski in the film and ended with a part of Mozart's *Requiem*. The response to the program was extraordinary. Many told me they sat for an age in silence when *The Science Show* ended.

Lisa Jardine died in October 2015. After that first meeting we met twice more and I like to think we became, and stayed, friends. Above all she convinced me that science, being a creation of fine human minds, is also infused with strong emotion, and this needs to be recognised. As her father implied, it is more than a torrent of facts. It is also a matter of history.

*

When I joined the ABC Science Unit in 1972 I met various members of the ABC's Science Advisory Committee. Several grandees of the field had been appointed as a flow-on from the very establishment of a science unit, a creation of three knights from the Australian Academy of Science plus the then chairman of the ABC board, Sir James Darling.

I was 28, had long hair and torn jeans, and thought, in advance of meeting Sir Gustav Nossal, that anyone with a knighthood and sitting on the board of a multinational company had to be a cousin of Beelzebub, whatever his record in medical research. He was then director of the famed Walter and Eliza Hall Institute in Melbourne, one of our Nobel factories.

Then I met him. Here was middle-European charm (he'd had, like me, a boyhood in Vienna), warmth you could feel across the room, an intellect like no other and that rare and precious quality so lacking in 2018: that this was someone you could *trust*. Over the years Gus has stood up for science at the ABC and in the nation. He was, of course, president of the Australian Academy of Science, and head of almost every other top organisation in the country dealing with R&D.

His advice has always been direct, fearless and worth listening to, and to receive his smile and handshake, which starts shoulder high and zooms across the room towards you, is an event worth bottling.

Gus was taught by that Australian genius Sir Mac Burnet, and his own contribution as a mentor cannot be underestimated. The names of those who did receive, plus those who should have received, Nobel Prizes for their work at the WEHI, go on and on. And he has done so very much for young folk in science here and around the world.

His research, like much of the work at the WEHI (Wee High, as it's fondly called), is on how we mount our defences against disease; how we marshal resistance yet can still tolerate certain foreign bodies without resisting too much. He has also led Australia's support for international work on health care with the World Health Organization and other bodies.

In 1999 I was asked by a newspaper to list Australia's top ten scientists of the twentieth century, and at first go I found I had too many from the WEHI. Mac Burnet had to be there: the journal *Nature* had called him a genius for grounding the field of immunology. Gus was there too, but for broader achievements, above all for leadership. So many teams and young talents gently encouraged, charmingly helped in ways that didn't make you feel embarrassed or put on the spot.

In 2015, when I was still recovering from cancer and chemo, I attended the black-tie dinner of the Australian Academy of Science. I had not touched alcohol for six months. Because of the chemotherapy it had tasted like sheep drench. But, now, having stopped the chemo (because it was killing me), I was beginning to recover. There was Gus Nossal, ebullient as ever, and he offered me a glass of champagne. I took it, out of politeness, expecting to lose it somewhere on a table nearby. But this was Gus, so I tried a sip, just in case. It cut through! Not a clear taste, but a flavoursome sparkle. Unlike the explosion in the head I'd experienced at Tim Flannery's launch, I could now once more enjoy a drink. I finished it and grabbed another. The magic of Nossal had worked once more.

Gus Nossal has been there at so many crucial turning points for me and many others. Like Derek Denton, Suzanne Cory, the Professor of Everything George Seddon, he may have been a grandee but he was one, as were the others, who transformed Australia and the lives of many of us in such important ways. Never forget your history. And never forget those who brought us so far in both an intellectual, cultural and, indeed a personal way.

The new meeja

'Tell me,' I asked the retired professor, an expert on word acquisition in babies, the renowned Jean Berko Gleason from the University of Boston, 'do children fail to learn to speak well if they spend hours looking at screens?'

'Depends,' she replied. 'Folk always condemn a new technology. In my day they were worried about comics.'

She's right. The Bible translated into demotic language would corrupt the masses, so the translators were burned alive. The waltz was seen as an assault on moral probity (a vertical expression of horizontal desires) and was banned; movies would debauch us — and video would kill the radio star. But we survived. We learned how to select what we needed. Stuff got sorted.

Now we have a global revolution. The slim device in your pocket (not mine) can put you in touch with everyone everywhere in seconds. It can bypass traditional media and give you a view of the world to suit your tastes. You can live in your bubble without having to bother about reality checks. At the same time nerds in faraway places can discern your habits, manipulate your nation's democracy, and undermine normal discourse.

Carole Cadwalladr of *The Observer* in London wrote about it this way:

I feel like I've fallen down a wormhole, entered some parallel universe where black is white, and good is bad. Though later, I think that perhaps what I've actually done is scraped the topsoil of the surface of 2016 and found one of the underground springs that has been quietly nurturing it. It's been there all the time, of course. Just a few keystrokes away … on our laptops, our tablets, our phones. This isn't a Nazi cell lurking in the shadows. It's hiding in plain sight.

She is referring to the algorithms that bring extreme right-wing bile to the top of your search list when you google a 'normal' question or reference about an every-day matter. She quotes Jonathan Albright at Elon University, North Carolina, who 'published the first detailed research on how right-wing websites had spread their message'. Albright said:

I took a list of those fake news sites that was circulating. I had an initial list of 306 of them and I used a tool — like the one Google uses — to scrape them for lists and then I mapped them. So I looked at where the links went — into YouTube and Facebook, and between each other, millions of them … I just couldn't believe what I was seeing.

They have created a web that is bleeding through onto our web. This isn't a conspiracy. There isn't one person who's created this. It's a vast system of hundreds of different sites that are using all the same tricks that all websites use. They're sending out thousands of links to other sites and together this has created a vast satellite system of right-wing news and propaganda that has completely surrounded the mainstream media system.

Cadwalladr reports that she found '23000 pages and 1.3 million hyperlinks'. Other similar reports abound. You have seen them. The net — and therefore our general media — is awash with distortions.

In October 2017 the *Financial Review*'s special supplement on 'power' put 'The Populist Right-Wing Media' at number eight in their list of 'covert' influencing forces, saying:

> By far the loudest noise in national affairs comes from this group. But the power is not direct. It comes from the way people with power react to their noise ... They have a big influence on key issues by airing hardline views which then filter down to influence policy, such as energy.

As ever these noises are blocking ones, raging against change, reform or environmental concerns. They are quite different from the enlightened conservatives of yesteryear when Richard Nixon paved the way for conservation in the USA and Prince Philip chaired meetings of the Australian Conservation Foundation. This is the paradox: high-powered media technologies are being used to mislead the populus and resist progress.

In September 2017, from the World Science Festival, I broadcast Linda Jaivin, just returned from a media conference in Hawaii, giving revelations about the firm Cambridge Analytica. She told how they used Facebook data that gave indications of a voter's general preferences and then bombarded them with messages to skew their choice in the direction of Trump or Brexit. Was there evidence that this made a difference to the outcome? I asked. She said there was and explained how this was tested.

I was surprised at the small reaction to this broadcast. Was no one listening? Did nobody care? Did they assume it was obvious? And then, eight months later the scandal erupted, Analytica was exposed and Facebook shares crashed.

What next?

Newspapers disappear, magazines fold, broadcasting outfits fracture, journalism fades and we end up ... where?

Books, I'm pleased to see, continue to do well, as paper or on screens. I and my fellow authors were surprised to hear this at an in-house seminar held in Sydney by HarperCollins. Books are not only being bought, but read. The older generation may lead this enlightened resistance, but plenty of youngsters are readers too. I met some of them at the Canberra Writers' Festival and shall never forget Emma who, age *eight*, likes to read military history. I talked to her about Florence Nightingale, who revolutionised the stats of mortality and health care in the field. Florence was, according to Chief Scientist Alan Finkel, not only the Lady with the Lamp, but the Lady with the Log(arithm). Nightingale was a mathematical whiz and her revelations pioneered epidemiology. Know the numbers, she averred, and you'll save many more lives than treating the afflictions afterwards. Em was impressed.

Mixing your media is important, not only for the eyes and personal relationships, but for your memory when young. The evidence is mounting that too much screen time in the first 12 years of life disables the skill of remembering. You get used to just googling life, not organising and storing thoughts and facts.

I ask my grandsons and other teens about this. 'Are you well informed?'

'Yes,' comes the reply, 'we have heard of the stories, the headlines, but know little of the substance. We scan, but don't read.'

Professor Susan Greenfield has written a great deal about these concerns and spoken in the House of Lords about them. She is demanding that more be done to clarify the situation as iGear becomes ubiquitous. Dr Ben Goldacre is one of her outspoken critics, saying that she should do the research rather than complain from the sidelines. The brawl goes on.

But where I work, on radio and TV, we have a new set of priorities — and a cacophony of new rather ugly terms.

I watch TV and hear radio at regular times — so I am *linear.* Those sources are now *platforms.* We all *podcast* and *download* and *share* and persist in *Instagramming* in a frenzied manner close to addiction. Count the people on the street or in the bus *not* staring at their iThing, *not* doing a thumb dance as if oblivious to their surroundings. And this behaviour has erupted only in the last ten years. Before that both the little screens and social media were hardly known. Programs about them are shamelessly about product-placement, noise raves comparing devices and servers and add-ons. It's like discussing motor cars without ever mentioning destinations and why you might want to go there in the first place. Why? Because it's easier to mention Jeep or Uber than it is to elaborate the wonders of Greece or Lake Tahoe.

At the start of this book I mentioned my stroll through the UCLA campus and seeing only one student out of nearly 20 *not* staring down at a screen. She didn't mind my remarking on her choosing to look at the trees and the sky and was perfectly friendly. I was on my way to see the great writer Jared Diamond. When I related this encounter to him, he told me that he thought the social and political instability in the USA was in many ways due to the hours per day (up to six on average) that Americans spent looking down at glass instead of looking up at real people. In our interview he said:

> The book that I'm working on now is on national political crises. I began it in 2013, before Trump was a significant issue, and already then it was clear to me that the United States faces big problems. The most urgent of our problems is our breakdown of political compromise, which has been building up since the mid-1990s, the political stalemate … but this is part of a bigger story. It's not just that Americans have gotten ruder and more uncompromising to each other in politics, it's more general; they've become rude and

more uncompromising in elevators, on the roads. Australian friends tell me that non-compromise is growing in Australia as well, raising the question why. And here we go back to what you and I were talking about, technology, younger people over the last several decades, especially in the United States, have had more and more of their human interactions go on at a distance, not face to face. You don't see, you don't hear the person. It's easier to be abusive to someone who is just words on a screen than someone who is two feet away from you. And so I see the growth of the non-face-to-face communication as being the ultimate cause of this decline of compromise in the US. But if that's true, then the rest of the first world is also going to get it. The United States will show the way, but I see this coming for other countries as well.

As for education: the Child Health Poll of 2017 found that Australian children spend 'at least four and a half hours every day looking at screens — and that's just at home'.

The way forward is to use the new technology in a way that enhances study and learning, and there is plenty of evidence on how this can be achieved. A major investigation by *The Economist* in July 2017 entitled 'The Future of Learning — how technology is transforming education', gave some encouraging examples of what's possible. Papers by Professor Rose Luckin of University College London back this up and even provide convincing arguments to show how new technology, properly used, can even do away with that bane of school and university life — exams!

Yes, reality is disarming, and disembodied communication makes for scary monsters. I often think back fondly to my cheery encounter that morning at UCLA. We should use the new media in combination with involvement in the real world, as Jared Diamond suggests.

The big question is: does all this technology fulfil a real need? Or are we being set up for this addiction by means of the biggest, loudest advertising hype in history that has thousands queuing all night outside shiny superstores for new models of iGear they'd bought only a year ago with money they could barely afford?

I say 'they' because I have never bought such objects. And when I go on tour professionally or overseas I am met with utter incredulity that I can negotiate life's challenges without these aids to omniscience. No Google Map in my pocket — I ask directions. I've usually looked up the way before I leave home. No phone at hand every moment — I can be reached when it counts and instant communication is essential only when death is threatened or dates may go wrong.

Besides, I am often thanked for prompt replies. My experience is that the people least likely to respond are those with the most e-addresses and devices to match. They are permanently distracted by bits of unnecessary business; too many messages.

The same goes for our broadcast media. Items must be short, we are told, and demotic and focussed on young people. It is they who are the next generation of consumers. Former ABC Chair Jim Spigelman found the label 'consumers' offensive when attached to ABC viewers and listeners. We are citizens, he insists, not consumers, and public service broadcasting, by definition, serves us. This was a topic we discussed at length over the years. I have known Spigelman for some decades and admired his commitment, first on the rides for Aboriginal equality in the 1960s, then to big ideas, most recently the importance of ancient Greece as the birthplace of so many essentials of civilisation, from philosophy and science to democracy and the law. Without institutions like NPR in the US, the BBC in the UK, and the ABC and SBS here in Australia, it is hard to see how these topics can be explored properly. I would include major outfits such as *National Geographic* and the Discovery Channel in this 'public service' list. Yes, we may be consumers of media products, but as citizens we need services that perform a different role. Leave it to the market and you will soon have wall-to-wall (or screen-to-screen) food channels, bonking channels (and I don't mean straight porn: count the dating series from *Bachelorette* to *Naked at First Date* and despair!), cop channels, weather channels ... and then dive into YouTube.

Brevity? Does the public really demand only short stuff? Well, it's interesting that the highest-rating ABC shows are one hour long: Richard Fidler's *Conversations*, *This American Life*, *LNL* with Phillip Adams, *Big Ideas*, (dare I mention *The Science Show*?), and the marvellous *Music Show*. *Four Corners* is 45 minutes, and half hours such as *All in the Mind*, *Australian Story*, *Off Track*, the former *Catalyst* and *Quantum*, *AM* and *PM* and the News are also substantial.

Putting all the tech aside for a moment, how would you revive a creative media ferment? Science gives a clue, so does theatre. Look around on campuses and clubs for little mobs of sparky talent, lively (young) people full of ideas and momentum. Think back to the crowd at Footlights in Cambridge (John Cleese, Graham Chapman, Emma Thompson, Stephen Fry, Hugh Laurie), the Chasers, the Pram Factory, the D Generation, then the various collections of science smarts being gathered in places such as the Perimeter Institute in Canada and the Salk Institute in California and you can feel the buzz as innovation takes off. I saw this in late 2016 at the Francis Crick Institute in London where the director, Nobel laureate Sir Paul Nurse, leapt from his tiny office to show me his new recruits, who had been hired on the basis that you 'select the best you can find and let them get on with it'. The very architecture of these institutes encourages friendly encounters (not formal meetings) and collegial interplay — few lifts, corridors as lounges where you stop and chat.

Instead, media moguls throughout the land meet in arid enclosures with killer powerpoints and plot restructures that involve deploying and firing many they never see face to face and putting out press releases about a new age of diversity and reach.

And it doesn't work. The figures are dire. So, more sheddings are required. Then new moguls.

*

In 1995 in Oxford, I wrote a slim volume called *Normal Service Won't Be Resumed*. It was a combination of brainstorming and finger-wagging — Cassandra meets *Doctor Who*. My predictions included the rise of programs on demand, instead of at scheduled broadcast times. The technology was on the horizon and while still a student my French nephew Frederic, my brother Shwn's son, was at the ABC as an intern doing the computer wizardry to make podcasting possible. So it was that *The Science Show* was one of the very first to enable podding.

I also, in my book, pictured a person on a train with a device that could download books from a satellite so you could read what you liked and preserve any jottings you made on the screen as you would in the margins of a real paper book. I told the dons at Oxford my vision of the future of publishing and they were astounded and even excited. It was their first glimpse (and mine through imagination) of what I later encountered as a Kindle. It's easy to conjure possibilities, but what about impacts?

In the 1990s we were, as ever, expecting cuts at the ABC and when I arrived back from Oxford with my manuscript of *Normal Service*, the Howard government duly chopped 12 per cent off our budget. We were going to shed once more. I look back in amazement now to the times when we could advertise for smart young talent to be science communicators and hire them. They would come with their own expertise in the new media and so we could apply it as needed. Now, instead, managers hire tech-wise people without the added skills in writing or performing. It's a bit like employing a calligrapher instead of Shakespeare if you wanted to write a play or a typewriter repairman instead of George Orwell if you wanted to produce a novel. We proliferate the signals but have not as much to say.

Then, in 2017, a breakthrough. Jonathan Webb, our new science editor, managed to recruit five new reporters for online science. They will, I hope, have the chance to broaden their skills across those 'platforms' as we did as a matter of routine previously.

Are we missing out? The answer is easy to test. Every year, thanks to the University of New South Wales, the Science Unit advertises for scientists under the age of 40 to join us for two weeks. We get hundreds of applications and could appoint most of them, the quality's so good. This reminds me of the days when we advertised similarly for new staff and, after competitive sorting, found Norman Swan, Peter Hunt, Alan Saunders, Natasha Mitchell, Paul Willis, Mark Horstman and many more. Each brought a wealth of skills as well as their fine intellects and incipient broadcasting talent. They were allowed to grow and innovate and surprise us. They were also, as are the five interns, in touch with a new demographic and new ways to solve problems. They enriched our culture in ways that gizmos alone cannot.

Natasha presented *All in the Mind* for many years and established it as a top-rating, intellectually rigorous show, a success on which Lynne Malcolm has built, giving the broadcast an audience of millions. Then Natasha moved on to *Life Matters*, a daily program on Radio National, ending her stint only on winning a Knight Fellowship at Harvard. Now she is back in the Science Unit producing podcasts called *Science Friction* on ticklish issues in research. Not bad for a girl from Melbourne who studied engineering.

Mark Horstman was a field academic, an ecologist. His splendid voice and acute intelligence made him a compelling reporter both on radio and, for many years, on *Catalyst*. I shall never forget his mesmerising show from Africa showing how knowledge of the original human genome, possibly still displayed by an ancient tribe, could reveal why diseases such as prostate cancer are so prevalent. Paul Willis was a palaeontologist (still is) and after years doing almost everything with us on air, was enlisted to head the RiAus (the Royal Institution of Australia, Australia's national science hub) and its Science Channel, and is now back at university.

Three stars, and there are many more out there waiting to be recruited if given the chance. I suspect that today I would not even make it past the first cull.

Yes, the new technologies are powerful and we could not do without them. But they produce too much collateral damage to be an unmixed blessing. Jared Diamond bemoaned the new lack of nuance and compromise in American society. He blames the isolation from which too many, young and old, are now able to send messages without the calming effect of a person there in front of them. He says many adults check messages every four minutes. If so, this is pathological. It is now well established as a type of addiction and, like poker machines, designed to give a dopamine hit every few seconds. Everyone says they are too busy. But with such labour-saving devices they should have plenty of downtime. What's clogging up life? I'll bet it's spam and junk.

About 98 per cent of the messages I receive are a waste of time. And I still have to spend hours sorting them. So do you. Communication, like politics in 2017, is a frenzied exercise in getting nowhere. Turmoil.

But what about all those individuals, clubs, networks, bloggers freed up by the limitless new technologies? Well, we all know that they are the usual mixture of good and bad: yes, keeping you in touch with friends, bringing you your preferred flavour of news, letting you know something a hundred times faster; but there is also the bullying, the shaming, flooding and distracting. People are now doing screen-detox programs — how many broadcasts have we heard on this theme? All that is beside my point.

I am concerned about organised information and ideas. The difference between Beethoven and cacophony, kd lang and noise. A few years ago, Mark Scott, newly appointed as managing director of the ABC, looked out of his huge office window on the fourteenth floor at the immense vista of Sydney and said, 'Out there are more sources of information than we in here could ever put together.' I and some colleagues took him out to talk about it. We said, fine, but our job, which is really specialised, is to do more than accumulate, we have to search and assess, analyse and report. This effort is what's evaporating. It's called journalism. But journalists, or pseudo-journalists, now write columns of opinion. They search screens, not the outside world. They don't leave the building.

Once you do leave the building the world looks different. It is both reassuring and terrifying, but in a natural way. It gives perspective. I once showed Mark Scott's successor, Michelle Guthrie, my shoes. To say they're down-at-heel would be an understatement. I walk everywhere and seek out the unlikely as well as the necessary sources. And they represent the extra part of what Nick Tomalin once said is a necessary set of abilities for a journalist (alongside a plausible manner, rat-like cunning and a little literary ability): legwork. Leave the building. Look at the trees. Now!

The new media were welcomed, at first, for two reasons. First, they were a gigantic new industry and meant new wealth on an incredible scale. Secondly, they are addictive and so made more profits every year. Having disrupted society everywhere, we must now, freely, choose how to use them properly: to enhance education, to bind communities here and abroad in revolutionary ways, to deepen communication instead of trivialising it, and to eliminate the waste caused by old-fashioned ways. This transformation won't happen unless we guide it and lead it. Just leaving everything to the market and the incessant proliferation of gadgetry is criminally lazy. Jean Berko Gleason is right: every generation deals with a fresh upset from new media, be it print, comics, movies or the screen in your pocket. Dealing with ours is now overdue.

But one final thought. When she became managing director of the ABC, Michelle Guthrie announced that her daughters, being quite young, would never think of turning on a decrepit machine called a *television* to watch a program. The word 'radio' didn't even arise. Guthrie added that the ABC has reasonable audience figures in retirement homes and nurseries. So, the question arises: are the likes of me being thrown into the ash can of history by those who've never heard of what we do and who we are?

Are we being killed by proud ignorance?

The fact remains that people talk to people and print reads as words, whether they're transported by electrons, waves or paper. The medium is not the message. The new media — or really new gadgets — are fine for giving us alerts, headlines, one-liners or two pars, which is just about all most people read, according to the research. But they are not good for deep consideration or thinking. We still need books, journals, even newspapers, of a kind suited to the new century.

Young people don't have the time? Bollocks! Half the time they're playing silly buggers. I've watched them.

Now what? More turmoil?

So where are we now?

Democracy looks to be in ruins. People are no longer as cuddly and enlightened as the Age of Aquarius had us hope back in the 1970s. The new media are destroying the TV, radio and newspapers most of us Methuselahs adore and the main activity at the ABC is farewell parties preceded by HR warnings about drinking responsibly on the premises. If Trump does something preposterous and the wise critics pounce, he just sends out an outrageous tweet about something else and the world, at least the herd, forgets the bad act and stampedes after the distraction like the silly tomcat in a Tom and Jerry cartoon.

Pauline Hanson has returned and will be around for a longish time. Someone once said (was it me?) that 'Australia needs Pauline Hanson like a hang glider needs laxatives.'

However, it's not really like that. The veneer seems appalling and the situation hopeless, but try another vantage point from which to contemplate the global mess.

At the last American presidential election only half of those eligible to vote were registered. Of those registered only half bothered to turn out. So only a quarter of the Americans who could, actually exercised their democratic right. Of those a majority voted for Hillary and not for the Donald — she had an extra 3 million votes. It is the weird American system that's at fault, not the nature of the men and women who live there. This is especially the case with the state system which, as I've already mentioned, distorts the people's choice, at least numerically. Democracy is not in ruins, nor is the majority unwise. Just misrepresented.

The interference from Russia and other possible gremlins won't last. Now we know it is happening, clever protectors will put up safety screens. Or else! But democracy must be *seen* to work — and that's a job for scientists as well as space-age psephologists. Edith Cowan has a university department specialising in protecting everything from home computers to bank accounts, as do many other universities. In a short while they will and should be able to vet the outcome of voting systems everywhere and to assess results swiftly to give confidence to a battered electorate.

No more hanging chads as happened in Florida in the 2000 election — if Al Gore had won, there would have been no Iraq invasion in 2003. If voters in key states had not been misled about their requirements for identification in the 2016 presidential election, expert observers say that the result would have been quite different. The people are not being heard.

Which brings me to the Brits wanting Brexit. If the US election does not indicate that Americans are sons and daughters of the Devil, a basket of deplorables, what does Brexit show? Well, Sir Keith Thomas at Oxford put it succinctly. He said that any organisation of any size, starting with your local tennis club, let alone a nation when deciding on a change to its very constitution, should *never* do so on the basis of a simple majority vote. If the Conservative Party had any sophistication (or shall I say: not been so bloody lazy) it would have demanded a 63 per cent majority vote to be the test — this was not an exercise in market approval, but a choice about a massive turning point in history. You don't want *half the population* to be pissed off. There is no doubt that some of the Brexit vote was an unthinking V-sign to the establishment. And now look at the immense waste of time, energy and airfares it's going to cost, let alone another election, to get the mess sorted.

God forbid if the West Australians with GST gripes really get stroppy and demand a WA-exit or Waxit. That would really be an experience.

I say all this not as a political commentator, I wouldn't dare, but as someone who has had a lot to do with the science of human behaviour. Once the electorate thinks it's wasting its time because the system's rigged or the choice of candidate is rotten, it (we) gets angry and cynical. The result is turmoil and you know it well. It is the flavour of our times.

It is traditional (that word again) for the left to have an over-optimistic regard for humanity, as Jesus did, oddly enough, and the right, let's call him Nigel or Osama, to think we're all a step away from villainy and must be thwarted. So, are we mostly bad or potentially so? Do we need constant vigilance against violence or pillage? (As I've said elsewhere: it is incongruous that this same right, in the same breath, stands, as Mel

Gibson would shout, for *freedom*!) Or are the vast majority of us pleasant and peaceful if allowed to be so? My
family certainly is, as are most of the folk you and I meet
every day, every week and every year. Not a serial killer or
bomb thrower among them. The contrast between private life with its warmth and courtesies and the turmoil
and ghastliness of what's depicted in the media is total.
So why do we assume that the entire world is hostile and
arm accordingly?

In 2008 in Boston, I was invited to dinner by the
literary agent and publisher John Brockman. He is to
science what Diaghilev was to Russian ballet or Brian
Epstein was to rock royalty. It was a dinner of the stars,
and I felt embarrassed being the only one without a
Nobel Prize or a book selling more than 5 million copies.
The one guest I didn't recognise was the fellow placed
next to me, a youngish handsome chap who reminded
me very much of Simon Rattle, the sensational British
conductor with his wild mane of grey hair and intense,
expressive features. 'Steven Pinker from Harvard,' he
told me sweetly. Aaahh, I thought, further embarrassed,
I should have known. We began to talk about his field,
language, and, inevitably, of Noam Chomsky, from the
other Boston brain base, MIT. After a few sallies on
grammar being wired into the brain (Chomsky's line)
or not (everyone else's now), I asked Pinker about his
latest line of research. He was investigating the evidence
for violent behaviour in human cultures, whether we are
wired for aggression and mayhem as chimpanzees appear
to be, or whether we are able to put slaughter aside if the
need is not there.

Pinker said that the evidence of present times appeared to be encouraging. After the awful numbers of the twentieth century with world wars and industrialised killing, we seem to have turned the corner. Notwithstanding incessant headlines and ever-grim news bulletins, the overall numbers show a *decrease* in the numbers of deaths due to violence. His case is subtle and interesting and, coming from a professor of psychology, worth examining carefully. (*The Better Angels of Our Nature* was published in 2011.) These figures confirm that, outside Port Moresby or the Congo, aggression takes effort and is not useful (even counterproductive) if used too much. It seems to reinforce the idea I presented earlier, that violence as policy is a product of culture combined with chaos. We do have alternatives if we care to choose them.

Angels has been criticised in many ways, not least for having too narrow a definition of who suffers from violence. But I will agree with him, notwithstanding the caveats, that we are more peaceful, overall, than the world I was born into in 1944.

Now Pinker has another book, *Enlightenment Now*, which takes the cheery news from Dr Pangloss even further: that science, reason and humanism have brought us, in nearly every category of human life, to a new, high level of happiness and fulfilment. This line seems to mirror similar sunny assessments from the likes of (Lord) Matt Ridley and New Environmentalist (!) Bjorn Lomborg. Pinker has been severely reviewed by his usual critics including philosopher John Gray. They suggest he has, again, used Pollyanna indicators that disguise dark trends.

But I am more concerned about those black swans such modern reincarnations of Dr Pangloss ignore. Those gigantic tipping points: climate, space junk, nuclear war, any big war with its metastases, ecological collapse — there are plenty of examples I don't need to list — which could change the nature of the game and press the button for greater turmoil overnight.

Nonetheless, in general, Pinker is right.

We hope.

So why does the opposite seem to be true? Is it because the thugs have worked out how to gain attention? If you want to be world famous tomorrow, you know exactly what to do. Take a car or a truck (you have limitless access), select a crowded precinct, preferably with some special cachet, and drive fast into the shoppers and strollers killing as many as possible. It is so easy. And the media will go nuts everywhere, even though the story is commonplace (as commonplace as a mass gun slaughter in the USA) but you will get headlines and a number one spot on the TV news, let alone Facebook, around the world. One nutter, one vehicle, one brainfart — result: global attention.

After the awful shooting in Las Vegas in 2017, Booker Prize–winning novelist DBC Pierre wrote an article about it for *The Australian* newspaper which, strangely, echoed my feelings. You may recall that his book *Vernon God Little* was about a boy with a gun who liked to kill. Pierre writes:

> Science tells us we contain strong, fast-acting
> chemicals, dopamine and cortisol ... and that

winners and losers are decided by these chemicals. That fear chemicals make losers and in the long term cause illness. And I wonder if, by being swept through screens into constant turmoil, we are priming ourselves with the chemistry of those who cause it, as well as promoting the market for worse … The business of humans is to meet. Guns allow us to forget. Screens allow us to forget … Stash our screens, take off our shades. Let our eyes meet and talk for real.

Pinker's version of a peaceful *Homo sapiens* has us embedded in a lively society with give and take, exercising the *sapient* part of our Linnaean name, not existing in fantasy land or in cyberspace where anything can happen.

You could say the same about politics. Stop the shouting. Stop the unrelenting aggression. Meet and talk. Plan for the future as once was possible: education, a national health service, even a fast train, as you once did with pride. But then Tony Abbott proclaims: the voter isn't interested in all that stuff about agility and innovation. They want retail politics. Make our electricity cheap again, as it was before the carbon tax made it double the price. The fact that we no longer have a carbon tax is irrelevant. Its ghost must be inflating our bills.

In Britain the left is pious but incapable. It has abandoned the art of the possible, of trying to get to govern. Now that the Conservatives have made a real attempt at harikari Mr Corbyn may fall into power by default, but not soon. In Australia the Labor Party may do the same.

Shall we spook the punters with dying reefs, extreme weather and CSIRO funding? Only quietly. Stick to retail.

I have two solutions, one structural, the other social.

The structural one draws on an important historical precedent. The first Labor PM in the world was in Australia. It was Chris Watson, who became prime minister in 1904. He did quite well. The only problem was that he was not Australian. He was from New Zealand. He, like me, never got around to becoming an Australian citizen.

Now it just so happens that most indicators (KPIs, if you insist) of New Zealand's performance are spectacularly good; the metrics are marvellous. I think, therefore, that we in struggling 'Straya should offer ourselves to the parliament in Wellington and from now on be governed from there. The third and fourth islands of NZ. Even the flag can stay roughly the same, perhaps with an added star on the blue and red. I mentioned this at a graduation address at the University of Otago in Dunedin and was touched to find everyone agreed it was a splendid idea. (I must note, hurriedly, that I made this suggestion many months before Jacinda stunned the world and became NZ PM.)

Malcolm could stay on as Liberal leader and continue to evoke past triumphs: re-empowering the Snowy Scheme, keeping coal top of the pops and strengthening our borders. I do hope he manages to get the Seekers back together again and gets (is he still alive?) Frank Ifield out there for the mums and dads in their cardies singing 'I Remember You'. Perhaps Malcolm would even consider giving Prince Andrew a knighthood — he did, after all, open one of our botanic gardens a few decades ago. Yes, make Oz great again, like it was.

Labor has a trickier job, needing to *do* something. But the party of the people has rightly eschewed the politics of the warm inner glow. Bill Shorten has perfected the cold outer snarl and could maintain the rage in public while NZ gets on with the proper tasks of governing that they do so well. It'll be tricky trying to keep out foreigners (we do allow lots in if they come by plane) even though Tasmania and the Northern Territory have populations less than those of Parramatta and Toorak.

As for Waxit — this could become a certainty if NZ took over the eastern bit.

I readily accept that the above may not come to pass. Which is a shame, because NZ is genuinely thriving and manages to be polite across political boundaries. (Their cricket is also going well.) The nation can even conjure up new political leaders overnight, as the NZ Labour Party demonstrated before the last election.

But the interesting point to consider about Australia's own incapacities is how a pioneering nation with startlingly enlightened policies, including being in the vanguard of giving women the vote (South Australia in 1895, following New Zealand in 1893) and the right to be elected to parliament. Then, after World War I, the nation kind of seized up. Why, according to Donald Horne, did this pioneering nation turn mediocre? Was it the lucky country effect — too many commodities and not much need to bother? Or, as David Marr suggests, was it the post–Great War effect of Australians identifying as British (if you weren't Aboriginal, or Irish, that is) and having a schizoid view of your real nature and heritage properly being elsewhere?

Shouting *oi! oi! oi!* and being cutely adolescent is no substitute for real achievement and it is a delicious coincidence, it seems to me, that at the very moment Donald Horne's withering critique was published, Australia became a real scientific colossus. After Howard Florey and the discovery of penicillin (deemed to be a British breakthrough and distorted by the dire intrusion of Scotsman Alexander Fleming), we had Mac Burnet and Jack Eccles winning Nobels and showing that Oz science rules, as well as the radio physics boffins creating an entirely new field of astronomy in Sydney and Hobart. Science in Australia at all levels, and in this respect it's not a cliché, is really 'world class'. The same can be said of Oz arts: the comedy, drama, films, music, books and dance.

Australia can be magnificent, if only she tried. Again! And woke up to recognise those whose names I have dropped throughout this book. They are equal to any nation's stars but they are not celebrated as such — despite brief flurries on Australia Day.

*

The social answers are more challenging. If I have any experience of anything very much it is of the wealth of untapped talent around the nation, and even outside it, waiting one day to come back or to be encouraged. They are as clever, as hopeful and as frustrated as any generation I have seen anywhere. I am a visiting professor at the University of New South Wales and the University of Queensland and visit other universities and colleges in every state. I put these young voices to air nearly every week and find the standard is stunning. They have also broadcast their troubles in getting stable employment once they have finished their 15 to 20 years of preparation in science or related subjects. We should be on the brink of a superb renaissance — as Malcolm Turnbull kept promising (briefly) with his 'most exciting times' riffs on becoming leader. Many of those young hopefuls are now becoming depressed; lots are broke. Why is there this profound disjunction between a population that embodies the hope of progress in the next generation and, on the other hand, a grudging and defensive leadership blocking the way and driven by the politics of grievance?

These young scientists and other hopefuls are the real creators of wealth, of Australia's bright future. That tricky word future again. The old standbys of coal, iron ore and agriculture are still keeping us rich, but it is worth noticing that medical technology is high up there, too. Brain-based goods are the way of things to come. This sector is already worth many billions of dollars. You know the list: the Gardasil vaccine, wifi, atomic absorption spectroscopy, plastic bank notes, pacemakers, bionic ears, ResMed apnea machines, spray-on skin and, in prospect: 3D printed nerves, muscles and jet engines; printed and painted solar technologies; bionic eyes; technologies to help the likes of crippled Superman and woman to walk again … So much. And there's the PM's prize for innovation which in 2017 went to Professor Eric Reynolds of Melbourne for dentistry.

Did you know that a milk-based therapy for teeth and gums is worth *$2 billion a year* in product sales?

We also have some rather large storms surging towards us. We need to prepare. If you don't accept that climate is likely to cause greater chaos I'm afraid you're in for a shock. History is unfair in that the culpable don't get blamed when found out. Who has caned those who refused to see that the environment, especially drought, may have been an initial cause of the civil war in Syria? Who is looking at similar causes for the probable upheavals in Kenya and Somalia? Why are leaders so blind as to see only political forces behind the turmoil? All we hear about are pirates and terrorists. Climate will unleash boat people from Eastern Asia on a scale worthy of a Spielberg movie.

*

The global challenge has been well summarised by Julian Cribb in his book *Surviving the 21st Century*. He gives ten 'intersecting' risks we face (I've called them black swans):

1. Ecological collapse.
2. Resource depletion — water, soil, phosphorus and timber.
3. Weapons of mass destruction.
4. Climate change.
5. Global poisoning: we are 'immersed in a toxic tide of 250 billion tonnes of human chemical emissions'.
6. Food insecurity.

7. Population and urban expansion.
8. Pandemic disease.
9. Uncontrollable new technologies such as artificial intelligence and killer robots.
10. Our capacity for self-delusion.

Julian, like me, is a former president of the Australian Science Communicators. He was once a PR man for the CSIRO. Now he is (like so many) a consultant and adjunct professor (UTS). His list has honourable pre-decessors such as science fiction writer Isaac Asimov's *A Choice of Catastrophes* (1979) and Professor Sir Martin Rees's *Our Final Hour: A scientist's warning — How terror, error and environmental disaster threaten human-kind's future in this century* (2003). All three writers are impeccable authorities and have been moved to make their warnings by their knowledge of the evidence, over-whelming as it is.

All three confirm there is action we can take to remedy the situation. Cribb gives two lines of hope: the first is a global brain, the second is women:

> Today individual humans are connecting, at lightspeed, around a planet — just like neurons in a foetal brain. We are crossing all the boundaries that formerly divided us. We are in the process of creating a universal, Earth-sized 'mind'. Through thousands of organisations on the internet and social media, tens of millions of people are now joining hands and sharing ideas, information, values and solutions.

And then, Cribb suggests, there's one of humanity's intrinsic problems:

> It is males, not females, who start wars. Who
> release the most carbon and toxic chemicals.
> Who clear-fell the forests, plunder and pollute
> the oceans, create deserts, slaughter wildlife.
> Males usually like to solve their problems
> quickly, by mechanical or chemical means —
> and to hell with the consequences. Men built
> modern society through the bronze, iron and
> computer ages, and that society is now at risk
> from its own success.

So Julian Cribb and I agree: we need an Age of Women to go with the newly coined Anthropocene. Julian agrees we may have needed the narrow, focussed, driven, typically male mind to push civilisations into existence over the last 10000 years, but now macho man has gone too far. He's taken us to the brink. In the presidential election of 2016 the USA had the fundamental choice between a male and a female leader and, albeit technically, they flunked it. The consequences have been stark.

In my book *In Love With Betty The Crow* I tried to convey the rise of female scientists in Australia and abroad. It is a magnificent revolution of the intellect with hundreds of brilliant women coming to the fore — all they need is the opportunity to do their stuff. Cribb, like the majority of modern men, is keen to see this happen.

We need more of the 'girlymen' one of our senior ministers keeps going on about, not more Rambos.

Julian's second line of hope is the wired planet. It will require the same filtering systems our own healthy brains perform with, otherwise the noise will be insufferable. But experiments with the wired city have already shown how this can succeed, getting running estimates of resource use, population, energy flow and air quality, plus ways to tune them if things go awry. Peter Rathjen, until recently vice-chancellor of the University of Tasmania, now vice-chancellor of Adelaide University, was keen to do this experiment on the Apple Isle and began the process while he was there. Tasmania is small enough, with a tiny population, to make such a scheme possible. It is feasible, one day, for the entire globe to be wired and, really, must happen anyway. Unlike our dalliance with social media and iGear, it will have to be more than marketing, a commercial splurge: we shall have to decide why we need Big Data and what we do and don't want to do with it. This difference will have to be like the wiring of our human bodies: invisible, prudent, forgiving and repairable.

All this requires massive dollops of goodwill from the 195 nations who will have to cooperate. At the moment there is little sign they are willing or even capable, though the 2015 United Nations Climate Change Conference in Paris (COP 21) was a breakthrough. A real crisis can concentrate the mind and there is a good chance, given the examples of the Montreal Agreement, the Antarctic Treaty (championed by Bob Hawke), and even the International Space Station, that a new impetus can be achieved.

*

The personal flows from all this. I have written about hatred because this Age of Turmoil has caused me to hate again in ways I've not done since adolescence. It is an emotion of despair. I have written about evil because it is a word of last resort, and I've been coining it more in the last couple of years. Hence, too, the preoccupation with failure. 'You are as good as your last program. Your last performance. So, watch it — or else!' And this is not a function of great age (grumpy-old-git syndrome) but being *of* our age. An age of turmoil and of failure. The test, the 'control', if you will, is the contrast with private life, which, for me and many others, is as happy as can be. Why this gulf, this abyss between the private and the public?

Not least with women. It occurred to me only recently, oddly enough, that I have spent only one year of my entire life living in a house without the company of women. Up to the age of 20 it was with my mother and, earlier in Vienna, with two very companionable nannies. Then, my first year in Australia, 1964, solo and, there-after with Pamela and Jonica. I have seen some men suffer badly without female company.

As for differing approaches to solving problems between men and women: I know one can trot out examples on either side to make any case you fancy. Rosa Klebb versus St Francis; the Dalai Lama versus the Wicked Witch of the West. Make your own case with random examples. But one which struck me recently was the contrast between a couple of science films by Todd

Sampson (whom I like a lot, personally) and my partner, Jonica Newby's in the last *Catalyst* series. Todd, for reasons I find incomprehensible, chose to illustrate some principles of physics by taking an AK-47 and aiming it at his belly, underwater, and pulling the trigger. This is in prime TV time, in the old *Catalyst* slot when youngsters are supposed to be watching. It brings a whole new meaning to the cod phrase 'Don't do this at home!' One imagines 14 year olds finding rifles and having a go and forgetting the underwater bit. Or perhaps pulling that trigger just a little bit too soon. His next film continued the same experimental do-or-die theme with a wrecking ball. They had trouble, I'm pleased to say, finding the wrecking ball. Had the ball weighing tonnes reached Todd, it would have crushed him to death. Macho physics, perhaps?

Jonica's contributions, of which I could cite several, had been an exploration of the substantial healing effects of music on the brain for patients suffering from Parkinson's disease or dementia (2016); and secondly, with some startlingly new research showing the positive effects of exercise when being treated for cancer (2017 — I was in this second report). Guess which of these four, the two from Jonica and the two from Todd, had the largest audiences? Let's just say that the AK-47 attracted less than a quarter of the audience.

Or take guns. Donald Trump — is this a surprise? — says that armed kindergarten teachers or maybe rabbis with Glocks would prevent the slaughter of toddlers or worshippers. Both sides should be gun-toting. Why not provide the kids with pistols? Meanwhile, Rebecca

Peters, a former colleague of mine in the ABC Science Unit, was interested enough in the effective control of weapons long before they became the scandalous issue they are now, to explore the best way of legislating to remove them from private hands. As a result, after the appalling shootings in 1996 at Port Arthur in Tasmania, she and her legal friends were ready when PM John Howard, in one of his finest decisions, searched for a means to get parliament to act. Rebecca had the paperwork prepared. There was no impotent standoff or prolonged obfuscation. After the necessary debate there was action. The nation changed. She has just been honoured, in 2017, with an Order of Australia. Now compare the figures for gun-related killings in the USA and Australia.

And in 2018, at last, in America, the kids are in the march against the guns.

*

So something needs to happen to enable people to work, play and live together beyond what seems possible if you look at the present mess.

First, the evidence. Despite the dreaded headlines, there is plenty.

Look at Sesame, a synchrotron now on line in Jordan. It is a collaboration between all the nations in the region — including war zones. A synchrotron is a big machine that throws X-rays at tiny samples of crystal to show their structure. When it was being set up I interviewed two people: a professor of physics from the Hebrew University in Jerusalem, and a brilliant young

Muslim woman from Egypt whose expertise in the field is legendary. She spoke coolly and with conviction. He spoke with passion, his Einstein moustache quivering. As I asked for some last words, he started to cry. She comforted him. Both were moved by a commitment to their science and their communities. Together.

I was reminded of Daniel Barenboim, who runs an orchestra made up of Israeli and Palestinian musicians. I knew Daniel in London when he was mainly a concert pianist of renown; he was an old flame of my wife Pamela's. In fact, we had dinner together in about 1967 when Daniel and the extraordinarily talented cellist Jacqueline du Pré were in the first stages of romance. He wanted to know about the merits of marriage. I gave him my considered assessment as a worldly 22 year old married for barely a year. I like to think he acted on it!

His Divan Orchestra, named after a collection of Goethe's poems, is made up of young musicians from all parts of the Middle East — Jews, Arabs, everyone. They play together with the greatest harmony, in every sense. The arts and the sciences: emblems of the greatest products of the human intellect and emotion, and also of the greatest international harmony and cooperation. It is innovation and creativity at its best. And it took a Jew from Argentina (Barenboim) and a Palestinian in New York (Edward Said) to make it happen. You do not need a 'burning deck', a Joseph Schumpeter set of disruptions like war and plague, to innovate in the twenty-first century the way we did during the first four industrial revolutions.

Joseph Schumpeter is another of my heroes, partly because he too came from Vienna. He had three ambitions: wanting to be the best economist in the world, the best lover in Austria and the best horse rider in Vienna. He succeeded in two of these. His ideas on disruption are applied by default today: a crisis is an opportunity, said Schumpeter, for us to innovate, to create something new and better. The trouble with this maxim is that turmoil nowadays has too great a cost: world war, massive refugee crises, climate upheaval.

We need collaboration, cooperation, international interaction and rather less testosterone. Except for sex.

Science and music, two of the greatest achievements of human beings and two of the essential ingredients of *Homo* becoming *sapiens*. Music and dancing preceded speech and enabled us to grow together in bonded groups. They are the glue of civilisation. Science and technology gave us fire and tools, so we could cook food and grow bigger brains. The rest you know. Both of these prime ingredients of culture show best how people can work together without turmoil (beyond a certain creative edge!) to face a trying twenty-first century.

Why am I going on about this? It is unseemly to have amateurs sounding off about running global politics. Or even office politics, at which I am equally inept. But it's different now. I am 74 and shall not see most of the dire outcomes, if they take place, that Julian Cribb lists so starkly. I won't see the turning points, good or bad, when they come. But I must say something about them while I can.

And: it's time. In 2017 the world marched for science in 54 nations and in ten cities across Australia. The potential for making good, for abolishing turmoil

is immense. We have the ingredients. The mild man-
nered have taken off their specs and, with any luck,
become Superman and Superwoman. This really could
be a turning point.

Acknowledgements

This is the book you write when you don't have much time left — or so I thought until Jonica stopped the chemo. The turmoil may be unabated but I hope I have retreated somewhat away from the brink.

My first thanks therefore must go to Jonica and my family, Tom, Jess and Pamela, who understood that I had to keep working, or at least, thinking, while dealing with the big C. My gratitude, as well, goes to those nurses and doctors who dealt with my decrepitude and tried to understand my jokes — and to Norman Swan who, once more, kept me on the planet.

My colleagues at the ABC were magnificent, and so very much so, was David Fisher, who managed to keep me on air, though I was lying there with a bag and a drip.

I made notes while in hospital and wrote as soon as I was home.

My friends at NewSouth Publishing insisted a book was possible and made many suggestions about how forthcoming it should be.

I have followed their advice and thank them for it.

Finally, I thank the birds who come to visit as I mull on the south coast of New South Wales. I know they think only of the grub I put on the deck to tempt them (and the possum), but it is remarkable how calming the constant presence of Australian parrots and corvids can be. And birds may safely graze …